Myths and Realities of Secessionisms

Miguel Beltrán de Felipe

Myths and Realities of Secessionisms

A Constitutional Approach to the Catalonian Crisis

palgrave
macmillan

Miguel Beltrán de Felipe
Faculty of Law
University of Castilla-La Mancha
Ciudad Real, Spain

ISBN 978-3-030-11631-6   ISBN 978-3-030-11632-3   (eBook)
https://doi.org/10.1007/978-3-030-11632-3

Library of Congress Control Number: 2018967761

Cover illustration: © Melisa Hasan

This Palgrave Pivot imprint is published by the registered company Springer Nature
Switzerland AG
The registered company address is: Gewerbestrasse 11, 6330 Cham, Switzerland

This essay is dedicated to the loving memory of Carolina
(1964–2017)

"M'he acostumat a viure / amb els qui ja no hi sou"
(Joan Margarit, "Ponent", *Misteriosamente Feliz*,
Visor Editorial, 2009—used by permission)

PREFACE

Since 2012 Spain is experiencing a difficult political and constitutional situation caused by the challenge posed by the regional government and by some local political parties of one of its territories (Catalonia). This government and these parties, backed by an apparently growing part of the population, are engaged in a secessionist process aimed at breaking ties between Catalonia and Spain, and at giving birth to a new independent state named the Republic of Catalonia.

I would like to make clear from the beginning that the legal and constitutional issues—and also the political ones—which surround the Catalan conflict are extremely complex and multi-factorial, as usually happens with everything related to nationalism, particularly to nationalist secessionism. From a juridical point of view, complexity might not be the correct word. The correct word is impossibility, because there exist only an extremely small number of countries, even federal countries, in which the Constitution allows unilateral secession. Apparently, only Liechtenstein (1921 constitution), Nevis and St. Christopher (1983) and Ethiopia (1994) would permit it. In the rest of the countries it is prohibited.

In federal countries sovereignty is enshrined in the Federation, or in the people of the Federation, and not in the States or Provinces. This has ordinarily been interpreted in the sense that only the Federation can decide about itself and, more importantly, that it is not divisible. See for example article 2 of the Mexican constitution, which states that "*the Mexican nation is indivisible*"; the Preamble of the Australian

Constitution creates *"one indissoluble Federal Commonwealth under the Crown of the United Kingdom of Great Britain and Ireland"*; according to the Supreme Court of the US (*Texas v. White* judgment, 1868), and based on the fact that article XIII of the 1777 Articles of Confederation had declared that the US union was to be "perpetual" and based also in the Preamble of the 1787 Constitution (which reads that it was proclaimed "to form a more perfect union"), the nation *"is an indestructible Union, composed of indestructible states"*, and therefore member States cannot legally secede; and in Russia, Chapter 3 of the Constitution regulates the federal structure, and article 137 allows its revision but apparently only to add a state or territory but not to permit secession to any of the 85 federal subjects (provinces, republics, territories, *oblasts* and federal cities). Non-federal countries contain similar provisions: article 1 of the French constitution 1958: *"France is an indivisible Republic"*; article 5 of the Italian constitution 1947: *"The Republic is one and indivisible"*; Portugal does not refer indivisibility to the nation or the state, but to sovereignty, in article 3.1 of the constitution of 1976: *"Sovereignty is single and indivisible and lies with the people, who exercise it in the forms provided for in the Constitution"*. And finally Spain, pursuant to article 2 of the 1978 Constitution, defines itself as a indivisible nation: *"the Constitution is based on the indissoluble unity of the Spanish Nation"*.

So in Spain, as well as in all the aforementioned countries, secession of a territory is not possible under existing constitutions. As I will address in Chapter 2, this has been recently ratified by three judgments of the German, Italian and Spanish constitutional courts regarding Bavaria, Veneto and Catalonia. In fact, in these three countries not only secession is against the constitution. A local referendum on secession is also illegal, according to the respective courts. Moreover, apparently agreed secession would also be prohibited—it would require a constitutional amendment, at least in Spain. Thus it is essential to keep in mind that Catalan secessionists have endeavored to do what has never been done before in modern Europe. I am referring to the fact that secession of a territory, and the resulting frontier change, has never occurred against the constitution and without the consent of the rest of the nation, or absent an armed conflict. This means that from a legal point of view, Catalan secession is not just a hard case *à la* Dworkin. It is a practically unviable case which has never come to fruition—but which nevertheless lays out some of the major issues of modern constitutionalism, and of course of politics as well.

The purpose of this essay is to explain the Catalan secessionist process, highlighting from a constitutional and also from a political point of view some of the problems that arise. I will begin by giving an account of the historical background of the Catalan claim for self-government and of the so called "sovereigntist process" ("*proceso soberanista*") or secessionist process started around 2010 (Chapter 1); then Chapter 2 will analyze the constitutional issues posed, and I will mention, from a comparative perspective, the precedents of the referenda in Québec and in Scotland and some similar problems in Germany and Italy; finally, I will make some reflections on the legal and political implications, including some comments on the mistakes committed by both sides, and I will give my opinion on the possible ways out of the conflict (Chapter 3).

Needless to say, given the huge number of recent publishing on the Catalan topic, both in English and in Spanish, I have had to select the materials and references, and to pick out only the ones (media pieces, op-eds and scholarly articles and books) which I have considered relevant or suitable for a non-Spanish reader. Any bibliographical selection is somewhat arbitrary, and this one is also deliberately incomplete. I assume in advance any criticism for the oblivion.

Ciudad Real, Spain   Miguel Beltrán de Felipe
November 2018

ACKNOWLEDGEMENTS

Earlier versions of this essay were presented in January 2018 in Oxford, at the Seminar *Sapere Aude* organized by the Association of Political Schools of the Council of Europe and in London, at the Center for Transnational Legal Studies; and later in May 2018 at the University of Oxford, in a seminar at St. Antony's College. I would like to thank the participants in these three seminars for their comments, particularly Lena Nemirovskaya, Yuri Senokosov, Inna Berezkina, Carlos M. Vázquez, Harald Wydra, Cristina Blanco, and Kalypso Nicolaïdis. I am deeply indebted to Prof. Nicolaïdis for the invitation to St. Antony's, for her warm academic hospitality, and for her invaluable recommendations regarding the publication of this essay. I am also thankful to the anonymous reviewers of Palgrave-Macmillan for their suggestions. Thanks also to Enric Fossas and to Francisco Caamaño for reading the manuscript and making extremely useful comments.

CONTENTS

LIST OF TABLES

Historical and Constitutional Background: An Account of the Catalan Secessionist Process

Abstract This chapter puts together the historical background of Catalan nationalism and secessionism, and the relevant facts that occurred in Catalonia and in Spain since the beginning of the so-called sovereigntist process around 2010. It tries to present the different actors (such as the national governments—Populars and Socialists, the Constitutional Court, and the secessionist leaders which have been in charge of the Catalan government since 2010) and to describe the main constitutional and political issues. Among these, the "*Estatuto de Autonomía*" passed in 2006; the judgement of the Constitutional Court which nullified part of it in 2010; the resolutions of the Catalan parliament which declared Catalonia a sovereign subject entitled to the "right to decide"; the "consultation" of November 2014; the (illegal) referendum of October 2017; the emergency intervention of the national government which dissolved the Catalan institutions and prosecuted its leaders; the results of the Catalan elections held from 2003 to 2017. The final part is an attempt of expounding the possible reasons which are at the basis of the Catalan secessionist bid.

Keywords Catalanism · Referendum · Catalan elections · Right to decide · Constitutional Court · Emergency intervention · Rebellion · Sedition · Unilateral declaration of independence · Estatuto de Autonomía · Convergencia i Unió · Esquerra Republicana · Popular Party · Socialist Party · Candidatura de Unidad Popular (CUP) · National government · Catalan government

© The Author(s) 2019   1
M. Beltrán de Felipe, *Myths and Realities of Secessionisms*,
https://doi.org/10.1007/978-3-030-11632-3_1

1   Brief Historical Overview

Catalonia, the Basque Country and Navarre (and, somewhat differently, also Galicia), are the regions of Spain which have strong cultural traditions and identity, and a characteristic history, and which have in the past reclaimed—even through war—a specific identity and self-government. Catalonia was a territory of the Crown of Aragón, which was a monarchy created in the Twelfth century, and was in the fifteenth century incorporated into the Crown of Spain—but keeping until 1714 a singular position of a certain level of self-government. After the succession war (1700–1714), in which Catalonia sided with the losing party (the Archduke of Austria), the new bourbonic dynasty which started with Philip V (grandson of French King Louis XIV) abolished the local institutions and rules (the "*fueros*") and centralized and modernized Spain. More than a century later, and again in the context of the succession to the throne of Spain, Catalonia, the Basque Country and Navarre started a war to defend their "*fueros*". The legitimate government, presided by Queen Elizabeth, won this first war (1833–1840), but soon there were other two wars (1846–1849 and 1872–1876), called the "*carlista*" wars.

These civil wars were not aimed at obtaining an independence status from Spain, but at forcing the legitimate government to accept the "*fueros*" and the relative self-government they implied. The rebel regions maintained that the Spanish monarchy had been founded in the fifteenth century based on the assumption that it must respect their "*fueros*". At the outcome of the "*carlista*" wars, and despite the fact that the rebel regions lost the three of them, the "*fueros*" were partially and indirectly acknowledged by King Alphonse XII: self-government was not admitted, but small parts of the "*fueros*" were recognized not just from a symbolic perspective but also from a fiscal point of view, at least regarding the Basque Country and Navarre. At that time (the second half of the nineteenth century) Catalonia was the most developed and rich region of Spain, it had an industrial and commercial bourgeoisie, and, as happened in the European political, nationalistic romanticism, stood up for its cultural identity as a nation. In the twentieth century there were two moments in which self-government was restored in Catalonia: in 1914–1924 (but with little real power) and in the Second Republic (1931–1939), with an elected autonomous parliament and democratic government. The so-called "Catalan question" or "Catalan problem" was one of the main issues in the first decades of the century. For example, the elections of 1907 were won in Catalonia by a Catalanist coalition, and in 1909 the so called "tragic week" caused protests, riots, burning of churches and almost 80 casualties, and brought down Mr. Maura's government. In October 1934, during the Second Republic which conferred to Catalonia a self-government system (through the first "*Estatuto de Autonomía*"), Catalan authorities unilaterally and ephemerally proclaimed the "Catalan state", and despite of the fact that this was much more symbolic that effective, it is considered one of the factors which led to the civil war which started 20 months later. Catalan leaders were sentenced for rebellion and sent to prison (they were in 1936 reprieved by the *Frente Popular* government).

Thus, at least since mid nineteenth century, a portion of the Catalan society, albeit being part of Spain, has had a strong identitarian spirit, and even a nationalistic vindication. It resulted in a political movement called "Catalanism" (see its concept and evolution in Juliá 2015). "Catalanism" —or, as Juliá suggests, "Catalanisms", for it is a somewhat broad notion that has many facets—is focused in advocating the political and cultural recognition of Catalonia, which would be obtained through self-government. Catalanism is based on uniqueness or at least on differentiation (the belief that Catalonia is different from the rest of the Spanish regions: the so called "differentiating fact", or "national fact"), on language (Catalan is a specific regional language spoken in Catalonia, and in Valencia and in the Balearic Islands), and also on a certain mythologization of the local institutions which existed in the past and were abolished by the Bourbons in 1714. The Spanish authorities, more or less democratic (from 1874 to 1923, under Kings Alphonse XII and his son, Alphonse XIII) or openly authoritarian (Dictators General Primo de Rivera, from 1923 to 1930, and General Franco, from 1939 to 1975), were highly centralistic, did not accept self-government (for Catalonia and for the rest of the regions and even for municipalities or counties) and did not allow public exhibitions of some of the cultural characteristics such as regional languages. In the three periods in which rule of law and democracy prevailed, even only for a short time, over monarchy or dictatorship (First Republic: 1783, Second Republic: 1931–1939, and after General Franco's death in 1975), political decentralization and self-government were considered a necessary consequence of democracy. Therefore, rule of law, and political rights and freedoms, were demanded for individuals, but also for regions such as Catalonia and the Basque Country which had a certain cultural identity, and even a nationalistic vindication.

2   CONSTITUTIONAL BACKGROUND: SPAIN AS A QUASI-FEDERAL POLITY

At the aftermath of General Franco's death in 1975 Spain started a democratization process, the so called "transition" which led in December 1978 to a Constitution which established a full democratic regime and gave access to Spain to the Council of Europe (1977), to NATO (1981) and later to the EU (1986). The constitutional monarchy and the Spanish state were based on both the unity and the diversity of Spain. Article 2 of the Constitution reads that

> The Constitution is based on the indissoluble unity of the Spanish nation, the common and indivisible country of all Spaniards; it recognizes and guarantees the right to autonomy of the nationalities and regions of which it is composed, and the solidarity amongst them all.

Political decentralization consisted in the possibility that "nationalities and regions", both under the name and structure of *"Comunidades Autónomas"* ("Autonomous Communities") could be ruled by self-government, with an elected parliament, an accountable government and constitutionally granted powers. It is important to stress that both the text and the intent of the framers envisaged two groups of territories: one group would be composed of the "nationalities", that is, the parts of Spain with a specific collective identity in which the demand for self-government was widely spread and which had previously had a self-government status. This included Catalonia (self-government established in 1932), the Basque Country (in 1936) and Galicia (also in 1936, although when the Civil War broke self-government had not yet been granted because it was only a project). These three historic "nationalities" would immediately and almost automatically become *"Comunidades Autónomas"* and be granted an autonomy regime (*"Estatuto de Autonomía"*) with a considerable level of powers. Actually, even though Navarre had never previously had a *"Estatuto"*, its status of quasi sovereignty from a fiscal perspective means that in practical terms it had a level of self-government similar to the aforementioned three.

The other group would include the rest of Spain, which in principle was not considered a "nationality": "regions" such as Madrid, Castilla, Valencia, Andalucía, Asturias, etc. in which the nationalistic feeling, or the aspiration to self-government, had never been clearly present or had never had a self-government status, or which had never had specific demarcations. They could also become *"Comunidades Autónomas"*, and be granted an *"Estatuto"*, but with an important difference: by default they could only initially have access to an inferior level of self-government, and if they wanted the maximum level (the one granted to "nationalities") they needed to hold a referendum with some majority requirements. So they were seemingly bound to be "regions", and this means that from a procedural point of view, the process to draft and sanction the *"Estatuto"* was less participative (because after being passed by the national legislature it does not need to be ratified by a local referendum), and from a self-government point of view it also means that the level and quality of the powers they could get were considerably inferior than the "nationalities".

The regional system framed in 1978 was an open-ended one. Contrary to other twentieth century European models (Germany, Italy, Austria) the Spanish Constitution did not establish per se the *"Comunidades Autónomas"* (their number, their name, their territory, their powers), but it only set up a process for their creation. So the political decentralization model was uncertain: the starting point (the Constitution) was deliberately ambiguous, or unspecific, and the resulting model was undefined, and even quite unfettered. Moreover, this process could hypothetically take decades, as had happened in Italy (four "special" regions, Sicily, Sardinia, Trentino-Alto Adige and Valle d'Aosta had their autonomy immediately granted right after the 1947 constitution, and a fifth—Friuli-Venezia-Giulia in 1963, and the other territories only acceded to self-government in the 1970s). Also, the level of powers could be asymmetrical, not only because of the difference between "nationalities" and "regions", but also because each one of them could decide the specific level of powers their *"Estatuto"* would grant them. Actually, the regional model was deliberately asymmetrical, given the fact that the constitution grants to the Basque Country and to Navarre a privileged fiscal status, similar to sovereignty in the sense that these two *Comunidades Autónomas* collect all the taxes—even national taxes—and they subsequently transfer to the national government a part of the revenue.

At any event, the *"Estatuto"* which creates the *"Comunidad Autonóma"* and establishes its powers is both a national bill and a regional bill, and pursuant to article 147.1 of the constitution it *"constitutes the basic institutional rules of each Autonomous Community and the State [the national authorities] shall recognize and protect it as an integral part of its legal order"*. It is drafted and passed throughout a procedure which requires in practical terms an agreement between the national government and parliament, and the *"Comunidad Autonóma"*. This agreement is particularly relevant in the case of the "nationalities" because the *"Estatuto"* passed by the national parliament must be ratified by an ad hoc referendum in the specific territory. This means that the "nationalities" (contrary to the "regions") have the last word regarding their self-government and can reject the *"Estatuto"* that the national parliament is offering to them.

Because the constitutional regulation of the *"Comunidades Autonómas"* was so open-ended, the political actors had a quite big margin to maximize the level of self-government, bringing Spain close to a Federal country, or, to the contrary, to maintaining it in a low-profile model, with relatively little political power transferred to the *"Comunidades Autonómas"*. They also had margin, at least in theory, to keep the constitutional distinction between "nationalities" and "regions", or, to the contrary, to establish a uniform model in which all the *"Comunidades Autonómas"* would have similar power—despite the fact that the framers' intent was to establish an asymmetrical system.

Very important choices were made in the immediate years after the promulgation of the constitution in December 1978. First, and contrary to what happened in Italy (or in France), the political decentralization process took only four years (the 17 *"Comunidades Autonómas"* were very rapidly created between 1979 and 1983), which is indeed a very short time, particularly if one takes into account that there was a military coup, Basque terrorism was hitting every month, inflation fluctuated between 15 and 20%, and political transition was not considered completed until the victory of the Socialist party in the 1982 general elections. All this did not stop the decentralization process. Second, after 1978 absolutely all the territories of Spain (or rather the main political parties) expressed their wish for becoming a *"Comunidad Autónoma"* and to have self-government (which could be considered surprising, for only a few of them had in the past declared such aspiration).

Third, and as a consequence of the former, during the 1980s and the 1990s it was apparent that the constitutional distinction between "nationalities" (Catalonia, Basque Country and Galicia) and "regions" would be practically nullified. The origin of this was an odd political event, when in 1980–1981 Andalusia wanted to have the same *"Estatuto"* as the "nationalities", that is, the maximum level of self-government that had been automatically granted to Catalonia, the Basque Country and Galicia. With the opposition of the national government, a referendum was held in Andalusia but it failed to reach the majority required. Andalusia could surely become a *"Comunidad Autónoma"* but not as a "nationality", only as a "region". Nevertheless, and after two legal ad hoc reforms of dubious constitutionality, the condition of "nationality" and the maximum level of self-government was also granted to Andalusia. In 1983 all the territories became *"Comunidades Autónomas"*, even the smaller ones such as Rioja or Cantabria with no clear previous regional identity or aspiration to self-government, and even some territories were substituted by national Parliament in their initiative to be part of the decentralized system or to join other territories in creating a *"Comunidad Autónoma"* (this happened to Segovia and Almería).

This homogenization was colloquially called "coffee for all" (*"café para todos"*), and it had enormous political and constitutional implications. The so called "differentiative fact" has been traditionally considered in Catalonia as an essential feature of the relationship between Catalonia and Spain—and of the Constitution. It was based on the implicit assumption that the constituents wanted to establish an asymmetrical system in which the nationalities from article 2 of the constitution would have a different, superior status to the other *"Comunidades Autónomas"*. That all the territories would become a *"Comunidad Autónoma"*, and that one of them (Andalucía) which had not previously had a *"Estatuto"* and was not conceived as a "nationality", was considered by Catalans and Basques as a breach of the non-written design of the framers.

And fourth: after 35 years of regional political decentralization, in which the level of powers granted to the *"Comunidades Autónomas"* did not cease to increase, the final model is very similar to a federal country. Ferreres (2014: 572) speaks of Spain as a quasi-federal polity. Starting from an open-ended, innominate model, Spain was de facto transformed into a Federation, also innominate. Each one of the 17 *"Comunidades Autónomas"* has its own elected Parliament, and its own institutions (government, administration), and some have their own police—and two of them, Navarre and the Basque Country, have in practical terms fiscal sovereignty. So the *"Comunidades Autónomas"* have significant political power, not very different from the power exercised by a German *Land*, a Swiss Canton or a Canadian Province.

Indeed, as Caamaño contends (2014: 81 ff.) there are some relevant differences between Spain and federal countries such as Germany, Canada, Mexico or the US. For instance, the judiciary, which in Spain is centralized, as well as criminal law (also centralized in Germany). The Spanish Senate is also not comparable to the *Bundesrat*. But the other federal features are quite clearly present in the Spanish "*Comunidades Autónomas*": predetermined, guaranteed powers exercised by an elected Parliament, including police and tax power. Apart from what Caamaño (2014: 243 ff.) calls "the spirit of federalism" (some democratic and accountability features which he considers essential in federalism and which are probably absent in Spain), one of the differences might be sovereignty, for Spain was re-founded in 1978 not by a sovereign agreement between the "nationalities and regions"—which did not exist yet—and Spain, but by the sovereign founding decision of the Spanish people taken as a whole: article 1.2 of the Constitution reads that "*National sovereignty is vested in the Spanish people, from whom emanate the powers of the State*". Sovereignty lies not on the different territories (the "*Comunidades Autónomas*"), nor on the peoples that form them, but on the Spanish people as a whole. Therefore, it was a devolutive, or top-down, sort of nameless federalism composed not of "nations" but of "nationalities and regions"—article 2, which reads that "*the Constitution is based on the indissoluble unity of the Spanish nation*", was interpreted as allowing only *one* nation and as prohibiting the existence of other sub-nations. At any event, from a political point of view, measured in the level of autonomous powers, it is clear that Spain can be considered an innominate federal country. In Chapter 3, Sect. 5.2 I will come back to this argument.

3   THE ORIGINS OF THE CONFLICT: THE "*ESTATUTO*" (2006) AND THE JUDGMENT OF THE CONSTITUTIONAL COURT (2010)

The secessionist issue has its roots in 2005–2006, when the "*Estatuto*" of Catalonia, which had been enacted in 1979, was substituted by a new one. "*Estatutos*" are both national bills and regional bills, and, as happens with the Constitution, their reform needs a specific process, much more difficult and different from normal lawmaking. In the "nationalities" such as Catalonia, regional Parliaments who seek the revision must send to the national Parliament a bill containing the proposal of a new text, where it is examined (and eventually amended), and once passed as a national bill, the "*Estatuto*" has to be ratified in an ad hoc referendum in the "nationality". For this reason, there had been very few reforms of "*Estatutos*" of the "nationalities", and the process of devolution of powers since the 1980s had rather taken place by ordinary parliamentary bills, or by decisions of the Constitutional Court, instead by amending or revising the "*Estatuto*".

In 2003 and 2004 the political situation changed quite dramatically. For the first time in the constitutional period, the national government and the Catalan government coincided in the same party (the Socialist party). On the one hand, Mr. Pujol, who had been in power in Catalonia since 1980 leading a right-wing, nationalist, not-yet-secessionist coalition (*Convergencia i Unió*), did not run, and although the coalition won the elections, they lost power to an alliance of the socialists, the Catalan republicans and another left-wing party. For the first time in recent Catalan history, a socialist (Mr. Maragall) was president. On the other hand, in the spring of 2004 the socialist party won the national elections and its leader Mr. Rodríguez Zapatero was elected Prime Minister with the support of the same parties that backed his party in Catalonia (*Esquerra Republicana* and *Izquierda Unida*). Given these circumstances, the socialists decided that it was viable to reform the Catalan "*Estatuto*".

A proposal was drafted and passed in 2005 by the Catalan Parliament by an enormous majority (a 120-115 vote), and was subsequently introduced in the national Parliament. It contained highly controversial provisions, which were generally considered contrary to the Constitution because they exceeded the constitutional framework of the powers of the "*Comunidad Autónoma*". Moreover, it included a bill of rights, which was unprecedented. Up to then, the standard of fundamental and social rights was established in the constitution, that is, at national level, and it seemed very problematical to allow to the "*Comunidades Autonomas*" to create territorial differences by passing a "*Estatuto*" which included a Bill of Rights. Perhaps the most relevant aspect of the proposal was that the Preamble stated in several occasions that Catalonia was a nation. As a result, the then-in-project "*Estatuto*" was quite similar to the Constitution of a Federated state. The opposition party (the right-wing Popular Party) fiercely confronted the reform (their leaders said that it would "rip up" Spain). Although the obvious exaggeration, the fact was that it was the first time in the constitutional period in which a territorial reform was to be made without a consensus between the two main national parties. This could be considered an implicit constitutional or political rule according to which the territorial design is an affair of state, which means that it should be fruit of a consensus at least by the two main political parties. Thus, some scholars and politicians, even in agreement with the necessity of a new "*Estatuto*", thought that the Socialist party should not have triggered the reform without a compromise with the Popular party. Mr. Durán, until 2015 a moderate member of the Catalan nationalist coalition which backed the secessionist process, acknowledged that it had been a mistake to pass the new "*Estatuto*" "with the support of only one of the two Spains" (2015).

During the debates in the national parliament most of the provisions of the proposal were amended in order to make them fit into the Constitution. For instance, the explicit recognition of Catalonia as a nation was transformed into two ambiguous sentences:

> In reflection of the feelings and the wishes of the citizens of Catalonia, the Parliament of Catalonia has defined Catalonia as a nation by an ample majority. The Spanish Constitution, in its second article, recognizes the national reality of Catalonia as a nationality.

This partial stripping down of the content of the proposal was not accepted by the most nationalist Catalan parties, respect to which the then-opposition leader Mr. Rodríguez Zapatero had created very high expectations by publicly stating in a party meeting in Barcelona that he would accept the proposal that would be passed by the Catalan parliament (in 2014 he acknowledged that it had not be a good idea and that he meant that he would accept a proposal of "*Estatuto*" which would be compatible with the constitution). As a result of the amendments of the proposal, *Esquerra Republicana*, the main ally of the socialists (both in the national parliament and in the Catalan parliament) withdrew its support to the amended "*Estatuto*". After the new "*Estatuto*" was finally passed by the national Parliament in May 2006, a referendum was held in Catalonia in order to ratify it. The turnout was relatively low (49%), and it was approved by 74% of the voters.

As all the bills passed in Parliament, "*Estatutos*" might be subject to an appeal to the Constitutional Court. It might seem odd that a "*Estatuto*" initiated and promoted by a regional parliament, passed by the national parliament, and ratified by referendum, and therefore which has been validated by the electorate, can be judged by the Court. Actually, the first legal regulation of constitutional adjudication—"*Ley Orgánica del Tribunal Constitucional*"—initially provided that the judgment regarding all the "organic bills", including the "*Estatutos*", would be previous to the passing of the bill and to referendum, but this was changed in 1985. Perhaps the fact that an *"Estatuto"* ratified by referendum could hypothetically be subject to a legal appeal might be better understood if it is taken into account the assumption that *"Estatutos"* are to be designed and passed after a political agreement between the main parties, so none of them would need to go to court. The fact was that in 2006 the Popular party, and some other regional governments in which it was in power, and which fiercely opposed the new *"Estatuto"*, filed a claim in which they asked the Court to invalidate more than half of the provisions of the Catalan *"Estatuto"*. It was the first time in 25 years of constitution that a *"Estatuto"* ratified by referendum was appealed to court, and it would have extremely important consequences.

It took four years—and an extremely harsh pressure towards the Court—to reach a decision. In its judgment number 31/2010, rendered in June 2010, a divided Court upheld most of the text but declared 14 articles contrary to the Constitution, and for some others it limited very much its interpretation. Regarding the declaration of Catalonia as a "nation", the Court stated that it was "legally ineffective", for it was not part of the *"Estatuto"* but was in the Preamble, and recalled that pursuant to article 2 of the constitution the only "nation" that exists under the Constitution is the Spanish nation.

The judgment was highly controversial, and in spite of upholding most of the *"Estatuto"*, was perceived by many Catalan political parties and individuals as an illegitimate attack on their right to self-government. The catalanist or nationalist parties contended that Catalonia had been ill-treated in two different occasions: first when the proposal containing the *"Estatuto"* reform was amended in the national Parliament, and second when the *"Estatuto"* was partially nullified by the Constitutional Court. According to this view, the will of Catalan people democratically expressed had been illegitimately and undemocratically amputated. A vast protest demonstration took place in Barcelona right after the judgment, in July 2010, gathering under the motto *"We are a nation, and it is to us to decide"* (in Catalan, *"Som una nació, nosaltres decidim"*) all the Catalan parties except two right-wing parties (the Popular Party and Ciudadanos).

This discontent triggered a process in which the nationalist parties retook power in the regional elections held in October 2010. Up to then the nationalist right-wing Catalan coalition (*Convergencia i Unió*), which had been continuously in power since 1980 (except for the 2003–2010 period), was not a secessionist party. It had been a nationalist, fairly moderate party, which represented the mainstream "Catalanism". Its policy at national level consisted in obtaining more and more power from the government in Madrid, in exchange for parliamentary support for the Prime Minister in the national parliament (this happened during Mr. González's fourth term, 1993–1996, and during Mr. Aznar's first term, 1996–2000). Before 2010, *Convergencia i Unió* had not openly vindicated independence, for "Catalanism" was not a secessionist movement but only a "regional" movement, the so-called "Catalanisn", nationalistic but allegedly momentarily satisfied with the constitutional framework—in spite of seeking steadily for more power for the Catalan "*Comunidad Autónoma*". As Keating (2012: 10) puts it, *Convergencia i Unió* had never vindicated secession, although it had been calculatedly careful not to rule it out in the future. But the "*Estatuto*" reform changed everything because it was other parties (the socialists) that had taken credit for the reform, and the power vindication seemed to be implicitly considered a dead-end, for the maximum powers Catalonia could seemingly get had already been obtained in the 2006 "*Estatuto*". This, added to the feeling of frustration provoked by the 2010 judgment of the Constitutional Court, provoked a substantial change not only in the right-wing Catalan nationalistic party but also in other minor Catalan parties: *Convergencia i Unió*, again in power in Catalonia in 2010, started to openly support independence.

4   The Uncertain Path to Independence and the Explosion of the Crisis (2012–2014): Vindicating the "Right to Decide"

The victory of the right-wing Popular Party in the national elections in November 2011, and the radicalization of the Catalan nationalist bloc, provoked an escalation in the political tension between the national government and the Catalan government. It is important to bear in mind that the Popular Party had strongly opposed the "*Estatuto*" and had brought it to the Constitutional Court, and that it had taken only 12% of popular votes in the Catalan elections of 2010. The national government led by Mr. Rajoy took office in January 2012 and maintained a very rigid approach to this matter. Following his party's fierce opposition to the "*Estatuto*", which it had appealed to the Constitutional Court claiming that it would "break Spain", Mr. Rajoy said it would not compromise, or even dialogue with the Catalan leaders: he would only "follow the law", and law does not allow secession, nor a referendum on secession. According to this view, there was nothing to talk about with Catalan leaders. These said they would in any case carry on their secessionist agenda because the Catalan people were entitled to the "right to decide". All this led to a growing feeling of angriness and anxiety on both sides.

Another vast demonstration took place in Barcelona, in September 2012, under the motto *"Catalonia, a new European state"* and with the support of many organizations of the civil society gathered in two associations called National Catalan Assembly and Omnium Cultural. Then the course of events hastened. After then-Prime Minister Rajoy turned down then-Catalan President Artur Mas' proposal for a new fiscal system for Catalonia (this system would be the semi fiscal sovereignty constitutionally granted to the Basque Country and Navarra), Mr. Mas launched a campaign which ended in a declaration of the Catalan Parliament that asked for a referendum or consultation to determine the future of Catalonia, and that called for the construction of a new state. Mr. Mas also called early elections in the fall of 2012. His coalition, *Convergencia i Unió*, won the election but lost 20% of its support. It is very likely that many of the votes went to a left-wing republican party, also secessionist (*Esquerra*). More than 49% of popular vote supported secessionist parties, and the majority of the seats of the regional Parliament (74 seats out of 135) were held by openly secessionist parties (and 13 seats went to left-wing, non-secessionist parties but who were in favor of a referendum): see Table 1. Moreover, according to most polls in 2013 55% of Catalans wanted a referendum to be held and 43% would vote for a full secession from Spain: see the figures in Page (2014) and in Robinson (2014). From then on, the Catalan political agenda was focused not on the economic crisis, or other issues such as unemployment or corruption, but on independence. The secessionist process had started (see an account of it in Galán 2013: 95–101 and 2014, in Boix 2017, in Plaza 2018, and in Page 2014).

The first step was a taken in September 27th 2012. The Catalan Parliament passed a resolution vindicating the "right to decide", defined in very broad terms as *"the imprescriptible and inalienable right of Catalonia to self-determination as a democratic expression of its sovereignty as a nation"*. By solemnly declaring Catalonia a "sovereign nation", secessionist leaders started to mix reality and aspirations, which since that moment has been the main feature of the independence process. In its first session after the elections, in January 2013 the Catalan Parliament, by a 85-41 vote, passed another Resolution nº 5/X "about sovereignty and about the right of the Catalan people to decide". This declaration was based on the principle that the Catalan people is a sovereign legal and political subject, and asserted that "Spain" had twice blocked the legitimate aspirations of self-government. "Spain" would have denied to Catalonia the "right to decide", and the Resolution allegedly tried to restore it.

The instrument for this restoration would be a referendum. In order to implement the "right to decide", the Catalan government announced a referendum which would take place in Catalonia in November 2014. The questions would be: *First, "Do you want Catalonia to become a State?"*. *Second, "If the answer is yes, do you want that state to be independent?"*. Aware that only national Government has authority to allow and to organize such referendum, on January 2014 the Catalan Government officially requested to the national parliament to pass a bill which would transfer this specific power. The national Parliament turned out the request in a 299-47 vote. The Catalan government now had one more grievance to add to the list: according to its political discourse, Spain was again illegitimately and undemocratically denying to Catalans the simple, essential right to be heard.

The Constitutional Court, and subsequently the national government, barred the referendum or any kind of substitutive polling regarding independence, but nevertheless, and in the midst of a serious political turmoil, the Catalan government organized a "popular consultation"—not a referendum, from a strictly legal point of view—on November 9th 2014, as the first and main step in what the Catalan government euphemistically had called *"people's participation process about the political future of Catalonia"*. The national government considered illegal the "consultation", and initiated criminal prosecutions against then Catalan President Mr. Mas and against some other high-ranking Catalan officials, accusing them of contempt and of fraud (for having illegal diverted public funds to the "consultation"). In the November 14th there was no official electoral register, and no public officials were present at the polling stations (instead there were volunteers). The turnout is difficult to establish, not only because the lack of electoral register, but also because non-registrered teenagers over 16 years, and foreign residents, were authorized to vote. The approximate turnout was around 37%, and 80% of the voters answered "yes, yes" (yes to Catalonia as a State, yes to Catalonia as an independent State), that is, voted for secession from Spain. In sum, there was a majority vote for independence in a minoritarian, symbolic, unoverseen "consultation".

The "consultation", notwithstanding the fact that it was a little more than symbolic and unofficial, was considered a success by Catalan authorities. Obviously, they sidestepped the low turnout and they exhibited it as a victory over "Spain", because they were able to overcome the prohibition. "Spain", they said, had tried to hush the voice of Catalans, but Catalans—ergo democracy—had prevailed. The "consultation" was sold by the secessionist bloc as a democratic victory over a non-democratic "Spain".

5   The "plebiscitarian" Regional Elections of September 2015: Victories and Defeats

By 2015, ties between national and Catalan governments were almost broken. In January 2015 then-Catalan President Mr. Mas said that he would again call for an early election on September of that year. But it would not be and ordinary election: it would be a "plebiscitarian" election, in the sense that it would be as similar as possible to the referendum on secession that had been barred by national authorities and by the Constitutional Court. It seems that the secessionist bloc was aware that it would be difficult to showcase internationally its cause based on a "consultation" a little more than symbolic, with no oversight nor electoral register, considered illegal by national authorities and not recognized by other countries or by the EU. A fully constitutional and legitimate electoral process—in which they seemed to expect a blatant victory—would back its secessionist project and provide it with both constitutional and political legitimacy.

The "plebiscitarian" election implied that the secessionist bloc would run united. This meant that all the secessionist parties, or at least the main of them, would not run with their own candidates, and with their own programs, but instead they would run on a united candidate list, which would include not only politicians but also members of civil society and which would not contain specific programs or measures but only the necessary political decisions to obtain independence from Spain—and the implementing measures. As they said, voting the unitarian list (called "United for 'Yes'"—*Junts pel sí*) would mean voting for independence.

The secessionist bloc made public a road map, based on the document issued by the Advisory Board for the National Transition, created in 2013 by the Catalan Government to give legal and political support and advice for the secession process. According to the road map, after the elections—which secessionists seemed to take for granted they would win—legal measures would be taken in order to create the institutional framework of a separate state, and independence would be declared within the 18 subsequent months.[1] Albeit the measures were not specific, this caused a breakup in *Convergencia i Unió*. It had historically been a coalition of two parties ("*Convergencia*" and "*Unió*"), and *Unió*, more moderate and demo-christian, and who had never expressly supported independence, left the Government and created a new party. It also caused some hard reactions on the part of the national Government: some of the Popular Party national leaders said the "plebiscitarian" election was contrary to the Constitution, and a political fraud, because it was illegal to convert a normal election into a plebiscite or referendum (which had previously been barred by the Constitutional Court). Precisely one month before the election, the police searched the headquarters of *Convergencia* as a result of corruption investigations. And the national government passed an extremely quick, non-negotiated reform of the Constitutional Court in order to allow it to suspend any official that would not obey or comply with the Court's decisions and to expressly give the police the power to enforce them. As I will explain in Chapter 2, Sect. 5, the EU played an unclear role: initially it tried to avoid any involvement or statement on the matter, but in the weeks previous to the elections the speaker of the Commission, and Mr. Juncker himself, made clear that they did not approve unilateral secession and that, in any case, the hypothetical new state would not automatically be a EU member state.

At that time, the principal problem seemed to be whether a super-majority in the Catalan Parliament (that is, a reinforced qualified number of seats) was needed in order to declare independence, or, to the contrary, if an ordinary majority (more "yes" than "no") was sufficient. In this regard, the Catalan secessionist bloc had not been specific. In fact it had been quite contradictory, because the "plebiscitarian" feature of the election is not compatible with the idea—expressed by Mr. Mas during the summer of 2015—that the needed majority for declaring independence would be a parliamentary seats majority, instead of a popular vote majority.

---

[1] See the political program, and the road map, in https://juntspelsi.cat/programa/programa?locale=es.

The main fact about the "plebiscitarian" elections of September. 27th 2015 was the high turnout, which reached 77.5% (booming from 60% in the Catalan elections of 2010 and from 69.5% in the Catalan elections 2012). Analysts and commentators debated about its effect on the final result. Some believe that this was detrimental for the secessionists: they were already mobilized (in several massive demonstrations organized since 2010 and in the 2014 "consultation"), and now it was anti-secessionist who mobilized to give a protest vote against Mr. Mas and the unitarian list—and against secession. Other argue that both sides (secessionists and unionists) mobilized equally and that the outcome reveals the actual social and political divided reality of Catalonia.

The outcome can fairly be considered a failure for Mr. Mas and the secessionists. If—as the secessionists insisted—it was a plebiscite (a yes/no vote regarding independence), then the secessionist bloc formed by *Convergencia* and *Esquerra* under a unitarian candidate list lost the plebiscite. As Table 1 shows, a vast minority of voters (47.8%) supported independence. 47.8% would be the result of adding 39.6% obtained by the unitarian list and 8.2% obtained by an extreme-left, Bolivarian, anti-capitalist, grass-root movement, the CUP (*Candidaturas de Unidad Popular*), also secessionist. Needless to say, a 47.8% popular vote support in a referendum on secession is a failure—as was 49.4% in the 1995 Québec referendum.

So Mr. Mas and the secessionists lost the plebiscite but they won the elections. Technically in September 27, 2015 what was on the ballots were political parties' candidates lists. Well, the unitarian list obtained, as I already said, 39.5% of the votes, which means 62 of the 135 seats in the Catalan Parliament, 68 seats being the seats required to have control over the Parliament, or absolute majority. The secessionists won by far the elections, because the second party (a new right-wing, Catalan-based, fiercely anti-secessionist party named *Ciudadanos*—"Citizens") got 18% of the votes and 25 seats. Nevertheless, it was a bitter victory: in the Catalan elections of 2010, *Convergencia* took 62 seats (and *Esquerra* took 10), and therefore secessionists had an absolute majority. But the Catalan early elections of 2012 *Convergencia* took only 50 seats and *Esquerra* took 21, allowing again an absolute secessionist majority (71 seats) and, therefore, Mr. Mas could continue as President—but this pushed even more *Convergencia* to the secessionist option. In the September 27th 2015 elections, the addition of the two parties (the unitarian list) took only 62 seats (but the extreme-left secessionist vote went to the CUP, which got 10 seats). As Table 1 shows, it is interesting to compare the results of 2012 and those of 2015. In 2012 around 48% of popular vote supported secessionist parties, which controlled Parliament (*Convergencia*'s plus *Esquerra*'s seats equaled 71 seats, plus 3 of the ultra-left party = 74). In 2015 the figures were 47.8% (39.6 of the "Unitarian list" and 8.2 of the CUP) and 72 seats (62 from the "Unitarian list" plus 10 from the CUP—although most secessionists and some journalists and analysts added the 11 seats of a left-wing coalition named "*Catalunya si que es pot*" which supported a referendum but did not openly called for secession).

So the interpretation of the results was not as clear as it seemed. On the one hand, the failure of the "plebiscite" was undoubted—but only by 2.2% of the votes. It was the first time in the recent democratic history of Spain that such a number of voters expressed clearly their aspiration to independence from Spain. It was a defeat for secessionists, yes, but only by a straight margin. Actually, from the secessionist point of view, this enormous but not majoritarian support could very reasonably be read as a victory. In any case, no national government could disregard such fact. Disregard was more or less the attitude of national government's attitude: the day after the elections Mr. Rajoy said independence was clearly defeated and absolutely out of the political scenario. That is, he seemed to act as if nothing had happened.

On the other hand, the victory of secessionists in the elections was not as positive or clear as it seemed. Not having reached the threshold of 68 seats which enables a stable, majority government, the secessionist bloc (*Convergencia* + *Esquerra*) needed the support of some other party. The only party which could back a secessionist government was the aforementioned CUP. The CUP is a grass-root, extreme-left, anti-system Bolivarian coalition, and, most important, it is also secessionist, but it did not want to join the unitarian list and ran by itself. It was a clearly minoritarian option in the 2012 Catalan elections (3.5% of popular votes and 3 seats), but in September 2015 it multiplied by three its votes and its seats, and, as I said, the CUP was the only party that could eventually support a *Convergencia* + *Esquerra* government. The problem was that the day after the September 27th elections the CUP leaders said they would not support Mr. Mas for being elected President, and they considered impossible an independence declaration.

Both statements were extremely worrisome for *Convergencia* and for Mr. Mas. When the unitarian list was created by *Convergencia*, *Esquerra* and some civil society groups, it was agreed that Mr. Mas would be the candidate for presiding over the government—he had been in office since 2010. Now the only chance for the unitarian list to reach power was the support of the 10 seats of the CUP, but the CUP expressly refused to support Mr. Mas: its leaders stated they would never agree to vote for him as President, which they seem to perceive as representative of the old right-wing "catalanism" which had been in power in Catalonia for decades. This seemed to be the end of Mr. Mas' political career, for he had to step aside and let another person lead the Catalan government. In January 2016 the unitarian list withdrew Mr. Mas as candidate for President and nominated Mr. Carles Puigdemont, *Convergencia*'s Mayor of Girona (one of the four capital cities of Catalonia) and also member of Catalan Parliament. Mr. Puigdemont was elected President with the votes of the CUP (the CUP accepted him because he was not perceived as the political heir of Mr. Pujol, which had been in power from 1980 to 2003 and because he was more radical-secessionist than Mr. Mas). The Catalan government was in the hands of an anti-system, extreme left coalition, which was surely a nightmare for right-wing, catalanist *Convergencia* voters. As for independence, the CUP's seats were also necessary for triggering the so-called road map. Its leaders were also very clear: at the aftermath of the elections they declared that "independence was impossible", given the insufficient results of the "plebiscite".

The scenario was extremely complicated. As I just said, the ambiguity of a "plebiscitarian election" allows several interpretations of the result. First and foremost, secessionist counted as votes in their favor the votes obtained by a left-wing coalition (*"Catalunya sí que es pot"*) which did not openly support independence but which supported a referendum on independence. Thus, depending on whether these votes were counted or not, the secessionists did win the elections. I do not think those votes were pro-secession, but indeed they made the result very ambivalent, and they forced analysts and politicians to be very nuanced in their assessment—which hardly happened. And secondly, the main problem I mentioned before (whether for declaring independence the votes needed would be electoral votes or rather parliamentary seats) seemed to vanish immediately after the election, for nobody seemed to envisage a unilateral secession with only 47.8% popular votes, or with 72 parliamentary seats which would include the CUP—which seemed to refuse to follow the independence path, given the results.

So the outcome was not as clear as it seems. On the independence matter, the defeat (that is, an under 50% support) of the "plebiscite" could be considered a victory, by a straight margin indeed, for the non-secessionists. But secessionists, despite losing the "plebiscite", could be relatively satisfied, for 47.8% of the Catalan voters voted for parties which supported independence. Ten years ago, this scenario would have been a dream for *Convergencia*, *Esquerra* and supporters of independence. And on the government matter, the victory for the unitarian list was a very bitter one, for they lost the majority they previously had. Mr. Mas called for an early election in which his ad hoc coalition (the unitarian list) lost 10% of its support, and the majority in Parliament, and in which he personally was rejected by the only party (CUP) which could give him the seats he needed for being invested President. Nothing was settled—except the electoral verification of a growing support for secession and of a very atomized regional parliament.

6   Insurrection and Reaction (2016–2018): The Referendum, the Declaration of Independence and the Emergency Intervention of the National Government

As was said, in January 2016 the new Catalan Parliament chose Mr. Puigdemont as President. What could be seen as a success for his party was in reality closer to a defeat. His party (*Convergència*) had broken his 30-year coalition with a moderate, demo-christian party (*Unió*), it had lost around 25% of its voters, it was immersed in enormous corruption scandals (which provoked a name change in July 2016, into the Party of the Catalan Democrats, PDCat), and now his candidate, and party's General Secretary, Mr. Mas, was rejected and had to leave his seat. As a result, his party, and the Catalan government, depended on two left-wing, radically secessionist parties (*Esquerra*, and above all the even more radical, anti-system CUP).

2016 was the year in which the judiciary took the lead, as a deliberate option of then-Prime Minister Rajoy. As surprising as it might seem, one of his main characteristics as a politician was silence, or inaction, and let things go until some solution or settlement is somehow reached. So he decided not to take any political decision in order to appease the situation, and not to initiate some sort of approach or dialogue with the moderate secessionists, if any, and instead he focused his government's reaction in legal suits against the Catalan government and parliament. For that purpose, he used an ad hoc, controversial bill previously passed in order to allow the Constitutional Court to enforce its own judgements. As a consequence, in early 2017 Mr. Mas and some other Catalan leaders (including the speaker of the Parliament) were prosecuted, and sentenced, for organizing the 2014 "consultation" or by authorizing a parliamentary vote about some aspects regarding secession which had previously been declared illegal by the Constitutional Court. Some politicians and scholars argued that the mere fact of allowing a Parliament to debate and to vote a resolution should not be considered a crime, or in any case illegal, for the President was not taking part on it and, besides, it could fairly be considered part of the democratic functioning of an elected assembly. They did not go to prison (they were suspended for any political, public office for two years).

Simultaneously, Catalan leaders were preparing for the next step, based on the fact that there was a "democratic mandate", fruit of the 2014 "consultation" and of the 2015 "plebiscitarian" elections, to achieve independence from Spain. So 2016, or 2017, would seemingly be the moment of what the media had called the "train crash"—a direct, open and probably intentional confrontation between the two Governments, national and Catalan. Actually, the preparations started in the spring of 2017. On the one hand, the Catalan government officially called a referendum on October 1st 2017, and begun to by ballot boxes and to mobilize its supporters. On the other hand, the Catalan Parliament amended its rules in order to create an express legislative process which would allow an extremely fast procedure to pass bills, aimed at attempting to avoid the prohibitive intervention of the Constitutional Court and probably also at limiting or eliminating parliamentary debate. This amendment would be used to pass a bill to announce and to regulate the referendum (and possibly to declare independence). Again, the rule amendment was later nullified by the Court.

As political unrest boosted (not only in Catalonia: in June 2016 general elections needed to be repeated at national level), civil society prepared for the declaration of independence. By "civil society" I mean *Omnium Cultural* and *National Assembly of Catalonia*, two secessionists, grass-root, very powerful, and politically connected associations, whose leaders were at least as famous as the secessionist politicians. Political conflict reached the streets, and domestic spheres. What initially was a movement quite limited to political elites, and which had reached the streets in vast demonstrations from 2012, became present in day-to-day life (schools, families, media, business and corporations, etc.). By this three-phase evolution (politics-civil society-everyday life) I mean that daily coexistence started to became problematic in many spheres of public and private life, and this was completely new. Catalonia was a reasonably cohesive society, in which Catalans and immigrants from the rest of Spain had lived quite peacefully (and in which secessionism was clearly minoritarian), but in a few years, starting in 2010–2012, it became fractured and growingly confronted.

The triggering fact of the conflict was a vote in the Catalan Parliament, on September 6th 2017, in which a bill was passed calling for a referendum for 1st October, and in which the question would be *"Do you want Catalonia to become an independent state in the form of a Republic?"*. This vote was a deliberate frontal breach of the law and of the constitution, and of democratic principles. First, because referenda are a matter upon which Catalonia has no powers. Second, because the ad hoc parliamentary procedure had been declared void by the Constitutional Court. Third because the Speaker had been issued a warning that she would commit a crime (contempt and disobedience) if she would endorse or process such a voting. Catalan authorities were openly defying national government. And above all, and fourth, this was a breach of democracy because the referendum bill was passed using the aforementioned new procedure which allowed any member of Parliament to introduce a bill *in voce* (that is, without previous notice), which gave just one hour to the opposition to propose amendments (and only partial, not to the whole text), and which allowed no preliminary reference to the ad hoc official board for institutional guarantees (*Consejo de Garantías Estatutarias*). The Official Journal published the bill in only two hours, and immediately after that the Catalan government (convened in a room adjacent to the legislative hall) issued a Decree calling for the referendum and designating the Parliament's delegates for the oversight commission (again, the opposition was given less than one hour to propose candidates). The announced referendum would have fewer control mechanisms, no voter register with the ordinary standards (in the sense that the opposition, or independent persons, could not exercise any kind of oversight), and was not to be carried out pursuant to the ordinary electoral law.

For these reasons the session in which the referendum bill was passed was extremely controversial and passionate. 52 of the 135 members (the national, non-secessionist or unionist parties) protested and left before the vote, and the parliamentarians expressly warned the Speaker that authorising the voting would be tantamount to a crime, for it had expressly been prohibited by the courts - with the warning that authorising it would automatically be considered a direct contempt. The next day another bill was passed (the *"Bill for the legal transition and the founding of the Catalan Republic"*) in which, among other things, it was stipulated that if "Yes" would prevail (with no threshold of turnout, or majority of votes), independence would be declared within 48 hours and the Catalan Republic would be born. Both bills from the 6th and the 7th September 2017 are known as the *"disconnection bills"*, in the sense that they supposedly were breaking ties with Spain.

It would be almost impossible to sum up in a paragraph or two all the events that took place between September and December 2017, including the emergency intervention by the national government on October 27th which dissolved both the Catalan Parliament and the Catalan Government and called for elections (at Catalan level) on December 21st. The national government immediately filed an appeal to the Constitutional Court (which automatically stayed the referendum bill); it established a severe control over the expenses of the Catalan government (in order to prevent money being spend on the referendum that had been declared illegal); it sent police reinforcements to Catalonia, which searched businesses and corporations that could hide the ballot boxes, etc. and arrested 14 high ranking officials of the Catalan administration (accused of preparing the referendum); and 200 Catalan Mayors which backed the referendum and were willing to lend municipal buildings to locate the polling stations were prosecuted. On the secessionist side, the civic organizations were very mobilized: vast demonstrations took place, a general strike was organized (one of the demonstrations consisted in not allowing policemen and judiciary employees to leave an official building they were searching: this would cost a prosecution, and imprisonment without bail for the leaders of the two civic organizations).

2.315 polling stations were supposed to open for the referendum. In order to prevent the police from shutting down them or from seizing the ballot boxes, some of them (mainly those located in public schools) had been occupied since the Friday before. In effect, there was a judicial mandate to the police—both to Catalan police and to national police—to prevent or to stop the voting, previously declared illegal by the Constitutional Court and by other courts. On polling day (Sunday October 1st 2017) national police irrupted violently in around 300 polling stations, in some cases beating the persons who were inside or gathered in the door outside, and seized the ballot boxes. Some other stations were shut down without noticeable violence. The rest of the stations (approximately 86%) opened and functioned normally. Ingnoring the judicial mandate, the Catalan police did not collaborate with national police in evacuating the polling stations and in preventing the voting. There was no official, reliable voter register, because few minutes before poll stations would open, the Catalan authorities said that there would be a "universal register", which meant that citizens could vote in any station. There were evidences that some fraud existed (some people voted four or five times). There was no independent, reliable and public recount, and therefore the referendum did not meet the ordinary constitutional, democratic standards such as the ones established by the Venice Commission of the Council of Europe.[2] In any case, the Catalan Government announced a turnout of 43%, with "Yes" winning by 90 to 10% "No". As Nicolaïdis wrote (2017), it was a defective referendum—but it was successfully showcased by Catalan leaders as a triumph of democracy over violence and over totalitarianism.

Two days later there was a general strike to protest against police violence, and King Philip appeared on national TV to stress the disloyalty of Catalan authorities and calling for the restoration of constitutional order. On October 10th, as a consequence of the "disconnection" bills passed on September 6th and 7th and pursuant to the result of the referendum, in a speech in Parliament then-President Puigdemont declared the independence of Catalonia, which was signed by the secessionist members of Parliament—the declaration of independence was immediately suspended by its signatories in order to start negotiations with the national authorities. The national Government sent an official request to him to know if independence had actually been declared. This meant that then-Prime Minister Rajoy was ready to trigger article 155 of the constitution, which had never been used before and which contains extraordinary measures, and direct rule (in the sense of suspending self-government):

> If an Autonomous Community does not fulfil the obligations imposed upon it by the Constitution or other laws, or acts in a way seriously prejudicing the general interests of Spain, the Government, after lodging a complaint with the President of the Autonomous Community and failing to receive satisfaction therefore, may, following approval granted by an absolute majority of the Senate, take the measures necessary in order to

[2] See the 2006 Code of Good Practice on Referendums, at https://www.venice.coe.int/webforms/documents/default.aspx?pdffile=CDL-EL(2006)033rev-e.

compel the latter forcibly to meet said obligations, or in order to protect the above-mentioned general interests.

In the meantime, many corporations and businesses had left Catalonia. They did not actually move, meaning abandoning the building's head-quarters or relocating plants or staff, but they changed their legal and fiscal headquarters for Madrid or for other cities in Spain The two leaders of the civil society associations were sent to prison accused of sedition and rebellion, the chief of the Catalan police was also prosecuted for conspiracy and sedition, and the non-secessionist citizens—up to that moment non mobilized—took the streets in a massive demonstration against independence and against Catalan government.

When the deadline to respond to the request was to expire, on October 27th the Catalan Parliament solemnly declared independence, and proclaimed the Catalan Republic, in a voting which ratified the previous declaration then-President Puigdemont had made on October 10th. Again, the "constitutionalist" or unionist parties (52 seats out of 135) did not participate. The result was 70 votes pro-independence, 2 blank votes and 10 votes against (from a left-wing coalition pro-referendum but against independence). That same evening, article 155 was formally triggered and direct rule began. The national government immediately dissolved the Catalan Parliament and the Catalan Government, removed all their members and called for elections (at Catalan level) less than two months later, on December 21st 2017. See a critical view of the implementation of article 155 in Ridao (2018) and in Albertí (2018)—casting doubts on it was constitutional—and in De la Quadra (2018), backing the Government.

In the middle of an enormous political, social and legal turmoil the General Prosecutor accused the Catalan leaders of rebellion, sedition and embezzlement. Rebellion is an extremely serious crime against the constitution which consists, pursuant to article 472 of the Criminal Code, in *"violently and publicly rising up for the purpose of [among others] declaring the independence on any part of the national territory"*, and both its leaders and instigators shall be subject to prison from 15 to 25 years. Sedition is a crime against public order which consists in more or less the same behaviour as rebellion, but which is subsidiary to it: pursuant to article 544 of the Criminal Code, sedition is defined as *"publicly and tumultuously rising up to prevent, by force or outside the legal channels, the application of the laws, or to prevent any authority from the lawful exercise of her duties*". The punishment is 8 to 10 years—but 15 if the criminal is a public official. The crime of embezzlement (misappropriation or misuse of public funds) is punished with 2–8 years, depending on the amount of the crime and of the circumstances.

It is difficult to admit that the Catalan leaders committed rebellion, or perhaps even sedition, because these are crimes which expressly require "violence" or at least a deliberate "tumult", and neither ex-President Puigdemont, the Speaker of the Parliament, the members of the Government, and the civic leaders, took by themselves violent actions, strictly speaking, and it is also unlikely that they could be punished as instigators. This idea has been expressed by many criminal law professors[3] and by the former President of the Constitutional Court, Mr. Pascual Sala, who sustained it in a media conference in October 2018.[4] On the other hand, and reflecting the views of Mr. Rajoy's government and of most of the conservative national press, emeritus constitutional law professor Mr. Jorge de Esteban wrote (2018) that "violence" as for the crime of rebellion does not need to be actual physical violence, or consist in tumults or riots, for in his view "institutional" or "psycho-social" violence is sufficient for committing crime. Similarly, emeritus criminal law Professor Enrique Gimbernat (2018) stated that violence was not a requirement for committing the crime of rebellion because a rising aimed at declaring independence would in his view be sufficient. Regarding the other crime (sedition), the charges might be more plausible, for no actual violence is needed (the accusation against then-President Puigdemont consists not in committing violent acts but in having promoted demonstrations and actions aimed at preventing judiciary officials to exercise their duties). This politically controversial issue (in my opinion not so controversial from a strictly legal standpoint) will be solved when the trial will take place and judgement will be rendered.

So the most relevant Catalan leaders were summonsed. Some of them voluntarily appeared in court, and were sent to prison without bail, but Mr. Puigdemont, and other leaders, left Spain and settled in Brussels, in order to avoid being arrested. The Spanish Supreme Court then issued a European Arrest Warrant (EAW), which, in a somewhat odd interpretation, was rejected as to the count of rebellion and sedition by Belgian and, particularly, German courts (the *Oberlandesgericht* of the *Land* of Schleswig-Holstein).

---

[3] See a Manifesto published by more than 300 law professors: see https://elpais.com/politica/2018/11/22/actualidad/1542906522_501939.html.

[4] See https://www.lavanguardia.com/politica/20181016/452391371442/expresidente-tc-pascual-sala-rebelion-1-o.html.

As a result, the Spanish Court dropped the EAW, apparently because if Mr. Puigdemont was surrendered into Spain, he could only be judged, and eventually sentenced, for minor crimes such as embezzlement or public monetary fraud. See a critic of the German decision in Nieto and in Sarmiento: the former wrote (2018a: 166 note of the author: the correct text is "(2018a, b: 166)") that the judgement violates article 82 TFEU, the principle of mutual recognition and the rationale of the EAW, and Sarmiento (2018) considered the German decision "astonishing" and "flawed". A more nuanced opinion, in fact laudatory of the judgement, was maintained by Foffani (2018: 198–199), who from a more conservative, traditional vision of the EAW mechanism wrote that the German court was right when it critically assessed the reasonability of the accusation, interpreted the so-called "double incrimination" principle, and, accordingly, acting in lieu of the Spanish court, ruled out the crimes of rebellion and sedition, which allowed Spain to try Mr. Puigdemont only for monetary fraud. Eventually, some of the Catalan politicians returned to Spain and were immediately summoned. Part of them were sent to prison without bail, others could pay a high bail.

The situation was unprecedented, and very peculiar. The Catalan ex-President was semi refugee in Brussels and lecturing in other countries, part of his government was in prison (particularly Mr. Junqueras, the Catalan ex-Vice-President, and leader of *Esquerra*), and the Catalan region had been taken over by the national government. It was odd that the proclamation of the Catalan Republic (twice) was a little more than symbolic—and nevertheless then-Catalan Vice-President Mr. Junqueras wrote in the *New York Times* (2017) that the Catalan Republic was actually born, and was legitimized by the ballots. It was also more than odd that there existed clear evidences that there was some Russian interference (the Spanish then-Vice-President said that the government had detected pro-secession propaganda and fake news coming from Russian soil). It was odd that the electoral campaign was run from prison, of from Brussels, by the candidates of the two main secessionist parties (the ex-President and the ex-Vice-president of Catalonia). The reaction of the imprisoned or prosecuted secessionist leaders was desperate. Part of them acknowledged that the proclamation of independence had been merely symbolic (probably they said so to avoid being sentenced). Actually, in June 2018 a member of the removed Catalan government admitted that they had "played poker" against the national government and that they were bluffing.[5] In

---

[5] See https://elpais.com/ccaa/2018/06/09/catalunya/1528573971_502571.html.

November 2017 Mr. Puigdemont declared in Brussels that he would hold a referendum in Catalonia in order if Catalans want to be part of the EU (clearly he was angry with EU leaders for not supporting him), and the candidate of *Esquerra* said that national authorities had threatened the Catalan government to initiate violent actions ("with dead people on the streets") if they did not surrender or resist to the emergency measures.

The regional elections, called by the national government as a consequence of having dissolved the Catalan Parliament when ordering direct tule, took place in an extremely hostile and controversial political climate—which probably explains the very high turnout (79.09%). *Ciudadanos* (a "new" center-right wing party, born precisely in Catalonia some years before, and fiercely against independence) won the elections, with 1.109.732 votes (25.35%), but the secessionist parties had the majority of seats. As Table 1 reveals, the sum of *Junts per Catalunya* (formerly *PDCat* and *Convergencia*), with 948.233 votes (21.66%), *Esquerra* (935.861 votes, 21.38%) and CUP (195.246 votes, 4.46%) was 70 seats—68 being the majority. The result did not show relevant changes compared to the previous elections of 2015 ("plebiscitarian" elections), and hence was considered disappointing by national parties. One of the leaders of the Socialists (Mrs. Carmen Calvo, who would later be Vice-President of the Government), had stated that "ballots will normalise the madness and the nonsense in Catalonia". They seemed to believe that the unilateral declaration of independence, and the deep social and political division and confrontation would provoke, as it did, a popular mobilization on the unionist side and a high turnout, and therefore a drop of secessionist parties (similarly, but without the partisan connotation, Nicolaïdis had hoped (2017) "that the elections of 21 December will not further polarize the debate but instead help heal the divisions that are now ailing Spanish society").

Well, this did not happen. Moreover, the traditional national parties took a disastrous percentage (the popular party, on power at national level, took only 4.24%, and the socialist party took 13.86%). So in practical terms nothing had changed, and the secessionists regained a Government from which they had been expelled on September 27th, when direct rule was triggered by then-Prime Minister Rajoy.

After some political vicissitudes (such as the attempt of ex-President Puigdemont to be elected President and to exercise power from exile), a relatively unknown member of Catalan Parliament, and not member of PDCat, Mr. Quim Torra, was elected President of Catalonia in May

2018, and direct rule was cancelled. Mr. Torra's designation was highly controversial, not just because he was seen by many as a "puppet" in the hands of ex-President Puigdemont (considered by secessionists as the legitimate President) but also because media published some old tweets and journalistic pieces in which he had said that "*Spaniards only know how to pillage*", that "*Spaniards should be expulsed from Catalonia*", that they are "*vipers, hyenas, vulturelike, scavengers, beasts with human appearance who only show hatred [against Catalonia, its culture and its language]*", that the "*fascism of the Spaniards who live in Catalonia is infinitely pathetic and repulsive*", and that "*here in Catalonia there is people which have said 'Enough!' and fight for their ideas and for their country. People that do not look to the south anymore and look again to the north, where people are clean, noble, free and cultivated. And happy*".[6]

When writing this paper (November 2018), the political climate seems to be cooler than it was before, mainly because of political events at national level. In June 2018 Mr. Sánchez, the socialist party leader (and who was not member of the national parliament), was appointed Prime Minister after Mr. Rajoy was ousted in a no-confidence vote. Catalan Secessionist parties in the national parliament supported Mr. Sánchez, and some steps were taken to rebuild mutual trust and dialogue. Mr. Sánchez launched a possible solution to the Catalan problem (to resuscitate the original "*Estatuto*" of 2006, prior to its trimming the Constitutional Court), about which I will comment later. Nevertheless, the trial of secessionist leaders for rebellion and other crimes is still pending (some of them are in prison since the fall of 2017), and tension between secessionists and non-secessionist escalated (for example, when the former displayed and wore yellow ribbons, as a support for the "political prisoners"—alluding to the Catalan leaders in prison, in pre-trial detention—and the latter removed them from beaches, buildings, etc.). Tension, and street violence, reappeared on the demonstrations that took place on October 1st 2018 to commemorate (or to criticise) the October 1st 2017 referendum.

As a colophon of this first chapter, and in order to reflect the Catalan political dynamics, follow two tables about the secessionist support in Catalan elections and in referenda, and then a paragraph in which I try to show some of the possible reasons for this support (Table 2).

---

[6]See https://elpais.com/elpais/2018/05/20/opinion/1526832715_834690.html and https://elpais.com/ccaa/2018/05/10/catalunya/1525975949_763217.html.

Table 1 Secessionist support in elections to Catalan Parliament 2003–2017

Year	Circumstances of the elections	Turnout (%)	Pro independence votes	President
2003	Convergencia i Unió - CiU - still not pro secession	62.54	565.000 votes (17%) pro independence parties* with 23 seats (majority: 68 seats out of 135)	Mr. Maragall (PSC), supported by Esquerra Republicana and Iniciativa per Catalunya (IC) ("tripartite government")
2006	After the new Estatuto, and CiU still not pro secession	56.04	435.000 votes (14.8%) pro independence parties, with 21 seats	Mr. Montilla (PSC), supported by Esquerra and IC ("tripartite government")
2010	After the Constitutional Court's judgment of the Estatuto, CiU for the first time pro secession	59.95	1.564.758 votes (50.3%) pro independence parties, with 76 seats	Mr. Mas (CiU)
2012	After the triggering of the secessionist process	67.76	1.787.656 votes (49.3%) pro independence parties, with 74 seats	Mr. Mas (CiU) supported by Esquerra
2015	"plebiscitarian elections" after the November 2014 "consultation"	74.95	1.966.508 (47.8%) pro independence parties**, with 72 seats	Mr. Puigdemont (Convergencia – Junts pel sí), supported by Candidatura de Unidad Popular - CUP
2017	After the national government's emergency intervention	79.09	2.079.340 (47.5%) pro independence parties***, with 70 seats	Mr. Torra (Partit Democrático de Catalunya - PDCat – formerly Convergencia), supported by Esquerra and CUP

Source Own elaboration based on official electoral statistics

*I have counted as "independentist" parties who openly stand up for secession from Spain in their electoral programs or in their ideology

**A coalition named "*Catalunya si que es pot*", backed by *Podemos*, got 8.94% of the votes (367.613) and did not support independence but was in favour of a referendum on independence. I have not counted these votes as pro Independence

***A coalition named "*Catalunya en Comú-Podem*", a continuation of "*Catalunya si que es pot*", got 7.43% of the votes (326.360) and did not support independence but was in favour of a referendum on independence. I have not counted these votes as pro Independence

Table 2 Results of referenda and "consultations" in Catalonia 2006–2017

Year	Subject of referendum/consultation	Turnout	Result
2006	Official referendum for ratification of the new Estatuto de Autonomía	48, 85% (2.594.167 voters)	Yes: 1.899.897 votes (73.24%); No: 533.742 (20.57%); Blank: 137.207 (5.29%)
2014	Catalan self-determination referendum, officially known as "Citizen Participation Process on the Political Future of Catalonia" banned by national courts, by national parliament and by national government	Between 33 and 37% (2.305.290 voters)	Yes-yes: 1.861.753 (81%); Yes-no: 232.182 votes (10%); No: 194.772 votes (5%)*
2017	Catalan independence referendum, banned by national courts, by national parliament and by national government, and partially impeded by national police	Between 42 and 43% (2.262.424 voters)	Yes: 2.020.144 votes (90%); No: 176.666 votes (7%)*

Source Own elaboration based on official electoral statistics
*Because there was no official voter register, no sufficient public, independent oversight, and no recount with full guarantees, the 2014 "consultation" and the 2017 referendum do not meet the ordinary electoral, democratic standards and therefore data are not completely reliable (particularly regarding the 2014 "consultation"), and vary depending on the source

7 Why?

The main query is to wonder why some of the Catalan parties have since 2010 set the pace to an apparently growing part of Catalan society to derive from a self-government aspiration to a fierce independency vindication. In effect, official, reliable polls show that from 2006 to 2010 secessionism' support was between 13.5 and 19.4%. In mid-2010, after the judgement of the Constitutional Court on the "*Estatuto*", the percentage started to grow, then reached its peak in 48.5% in November 2013, and gradually declined until 40.2% in October 2017 (when the referendum took place), and the last data (spring 2018) show a drop (32.9%). But if the option of "a state within Federal Spain" is added, then support for independence climbs to 52.5%. Nevertheless, if the only two possible options are "*Do you want Catalonia to become an independent State?*", the result is Yes 40.8%, No 53.9%.[7]

So why Catalanism has embraced secessionism? Here are some of the possible reasons.

a. the so called "*café para todos*", or "coffee for all", that is, the generalization to all the "*Comunidades Autónomas*" of a very similar level of powers, and accordingly, the vanishing of the constitutional and symbolic asymmetries which supposedly differentiated Catalonia to the rest of the Spanish territories (see Sect. 2 of this chapter). This is a very important constitutional factor, and constitutes also a relevant psychological collective perception. It is not just a question of level of self-government, it is a question of having more self-government (and symbolic status) than the rest of the territories of Spain that are not a "nationality"—whatever this word means. According to Catalan (and also Basque) leaders, "coffee for all" means not just a breach of the constitutional non-written pact regarding the asymmetry between "nationalities" and "regions": it means decaffeinated coffee, in the sense that it is devaluated or insufficient. This perception grew overtime, and reached its peak in the mid-2000s, when other *Comunidades Autónomas*—particularly Andalucía—copied the "*Estatuto*" that Catalonia had promoted in 2005 and that was partially nullified by the Constitutional Court in 2010. Even more, as Presno stresses (2015: 4–5), the "*Estatuto*" of Andalucía contained provisions practically identical to the Catalan, but the Popular Party did not appeal them to the Court, and therefore many Catalan politicians and individuals felt, not without reason, that this situation was unfair and that the Popular Party was attacking them just for rancor. This growing dissatisfaction with the resulting constitutional decentralized system has indeed have spread secessionism;

b. the frustration caused by the trimming off of the "*Estatuto*", first in the national parliament in 2006 and secondly by the Constitutional Court in 2010;

---

[7] See Political Context Survey, 2018, of the Centre d'Estudis d'Opinió, from the Catalan Government, at http://upceo.ceo.gencat.cat/wsceop/6508/Abstract%20in%20 English%20-874.pdf.

c. the growing feeling—openly fostered by practically every Catalan government since 1980, and verified in many polls and surveys: see Grau (2011)—that Catalonia was, and still is, unfairly fiscally treated. The Resolutions adopted by the Catalan Parliament in 2012 and 2013, and the aforementioned white paper by the Advisory Board for the National Transition openly referred to "fiscal pillage" and to "fiscal plundering". It is the same discourse as the Italian "Lega Nord" (*"Rome is stealing us"*), and it reflects the unsolved issue of fiscal federalism. Since the beginning of the economic crisis in 2008, this discourse boosted, despite the fact that it is not clear at all from an economic point of view that the fiscal balance between Catalonia and the rest of Spain is actually as unfair and detrimental as the nationalist bloc suggest: see two opposed data in Advisory Board for the National Transition (2014: 65 ss.) and in Garicano (2015). Some economists argue that without the income transferred to Catalonia from the national government, for instance to pay the retirement pensions, Catalonia as an independent state would have enormous problems, notwithstanding the fact that it is one of the richest regions of Spain.[8] For a defense of the economic viability of a seceded Catalonia see, more broadly, Bosch and Espasa (2014);

d. the economic crisis started in 2008, which seemed to blame its causes and its consequences on "Spain" and its corruption—although corruption and bribery scandals have also reached Catalan parties and Catalan society. In 2015 Mr. Pujol, founder of *Convergencia*, and President of Catalonia from 1980 to 2003, was prosecuted for bribery and tax evasion (which probably conceals illegal financing of its party), and an ad hoc investigative commission was created in the Catalan Parliament. In any case, it seems as if a growing part of Catalans were channeling into "Spain" the angriness and exasperation caused by the crisis and the monumental corruption scandals. As Robinson (2011) puts it, a great number of Catalans felt cheated by their national governments' response to the crisis;

e. some sociologists say that there could be a generational reason, in the sense that many of the supporters of secession are people under

[8] See https://www.bbc.co.uk/programmes/w3cstydb.

40 who did not live under General Franco's regime (they have lived almost all their lives in the democratic system, and the youngest ones have only lived as EU citizens). Therefore, instead of being satisfied with the current status granted by the Constitution, or of being afraid of pushing up the secessionist movement, a significant part of this generation takes self-government for granted, and tends to believe the "Spanish" democratic system is severely flawed. In some way, they have little respect for the Transition and for a constitution whose crucial role in reconciliation and in overcoming General Franco's dictatorship seems to be disregarded;

f. the growing political power and social influence by *Esquerra Republicana*, a left-wing party openly independentist and contrary to Monarchy. Its parliamentary support was needed to set up majorities in the national parliament (in 2004–2008) and in the Catalan parliament (since 2003, both with socialist governments and with *Convergencia i Unió*'s governments). Moreover, after the 2012 elections Mr. Mas needed its support in order to keep the power, so he apparently had no option but to follow *Esquerra*'s radical political agenda. It is unclear whether a right-wing coalition like *Convergencia i Unió* would have embraced such a secessionist path had it not needed *Esquerra*'s parliamentary support—clearly left-wing party. After the 2015 regional elections, an ultra-leftist, radical, anti-capitalist party the CUP (Candidates for Popular Union) pushed ahead the secessionist agenda, for its support was indispensable for the coalition government of *Convergencia* and *Esquerra*. If they wanted to stay in power after the elections of 2015 and 2017, these two parties were literally in the hands of the CUP, which openly favors unilateral secession. There is an evident shift towards secessionism in Catalan politics, which has boosted secessionist parties, has led to some kind of fight for the growing independentist voters and has clearly put in the background the traditional right/left divide—and has left aside, in the secessionist side, virtually all the social problems and policies;

g. the last reason is perhaps a somewhat irrational forging ahead pushed by the main nationalist parties (*Convergencia i Unió* and *Esquerra Republicana*) in order to preserve their political discourse, and even their own survival, once a high level of self-government had already been obtained after 40 years of decentralization and after the new 2006 "*Estatuto*".

As happens very frequently in politics, some of these circumstances are not completely real, meaning that they are not fact-based, or that they are collective perceptions not supported by undisputed, objective facts. But of course the fact that they might be not real does not mean that they are negligible or that they cannot be the basis for a powerful social and political movement. It is well known that in politics "reality" is a different thing than in other aspects of life. In any case, this leads us to nationalism, which is normally based, precisely, more in affections, feelings or in identities than in facts or in rational logic. Catalan nationalist parties, and part of the Catalan society, have a strong nationalistic belief. As I explained in Sects. 2 and 3 above, in the constitutional period after Franco's death, and approximately up to 2007, self-government granted by a democratic regime temporarily appeased secessionist feelings—which in any case were clearly minoritarian. Juliá (2015) stresses that during this period (1978–2007), moderate nationalism or Catalanism was not a secessionist movement, or at least it did not push a secessionist discourse or agenda. But after 2007, and particularly after the 2012 regional elections, and because the aforementioned circumstances or because some other minor pretexts more or less real, moderate nationalism became more radical, and started to vindicate independence. A very relevant Catalan journalist, deputy director of EL PAÍS (the main newspaper in Spain) contends that this was a great surprise (Bassets 2015). As Fossas (2014) says, Mr. Mas succumbed to the insurrectionist temptation.

What I mean is that those circumstances have boosted an inveterate nationalism, impervious to constitutionalism, to democracy and to self-government. Robinson (2014) writes that in Scotland and in Catalonia there exists a desperate search for sovereignty by voters who claim to have longstanding resentments over discrimination by their states. And in effect, since the nineteenth century nationalism has always had this somewhat irrational root. The Spanish democratic regime, with its intense political decentralization, and its full integration in the EU since 1986, was not able to defeat myths, symbols, banners, and history. And the downside of nationalism and its myths has showed up in Spain in the recent years—in both sides, but particularly in the Catalan secessionist government, when it has equaled itself to "the Catalan people" and has started to use a primitive political discourse based on victimization and on a friend/foe dialectic, actually in many aspects close to demagogy or to populism.

References

Advisory Board for the National Transition. 2014. *The National Transition of Catalonia.* http://presidencia.gencat.cat/web/.content/ambits_actuacio/consells_assessors/catn/informes_publicats/llibre_blanc_angles.pdf.

Albertí, Enoch. 2018. Cuestiones constitucionales en torno a la aplicación del artículo 155 CE en el conflicto de Cataluña. *Revista de Estudios Autonómicos y Federales* (27): 1–23.

Bassets, Lluis. 2015. Tres sorpresas catalanas. *EL PAÍS*, September 1. http://elpais.com/elpais/2015/08/29/opinion/1440870537_660655.html.

Boix, Andrés. 2017. El conflicto catalán y la crisis constitucional española: una cronología. *El Cronista del Estado Social y Democrático de Derecho* (71–72): 172–181.

Bosch, Nuria, and Marta Espasa. 2014. La viabilidad económica de una Cataluña independiente. *Revista de Economía Aplicada* número XXII (64): 135–162. http://www.revecap.com/revista/numeros/64/pdf/bosch_espasa2.pdf.

Caamaño, Francisco. 2014. *Democracia federal: Apuntes sobre España.* Madrid: Ediciones Turpial.

De Esteban, Jorge. 2018. Rebelión o rebelión. November 1. https://www.elmundo.es/opinion/2018/11/01/5bd9aefc46163f13978b457e.html.

De la Quadra-Salcedo, Tomás. 2018. Reflexiones sobre el artículo 155 de la constitución y la protección del interés general de España. *Revista Española de Derecho Administrativo* (191): 25–76.

Durán i Lleida, Josep Antoni. 2015. A Felipe González…. y a los españoles. *EL PAÍS*, September 2. http://elpais.com/elpais/2015/09/01/opinion/1441123763_525687.html.

Ferreres Comella, Victor. 2014. The Spanish Constitutional Court Confronts Catalonia's 'Right to Decide' (Comment on the Judgment 42/2014). *European Constitutional Law Review* 10 (3): 571–590.

Foffani, Luigi. 2018. The Case Puigdemont: The Stress-Test of the European Arrest Warrant. *European Criminal Law Review* 8 (2): 196–200.

Fossas Espadaler, Enric. 2014. Secesión: del proceso eufemístico al constitucional. *EL PAÍS*, November 25. http://elpais.com/elpais/2014/11/24/opinion/1416842833_782695.html.

Galán Galán, Alfredo. 2013. Secesión de Estados y pertenencia a la Unión Europea: Cataluña en la encrucijada. *Istituzioni del Federalismo* (1): 95–135.

Galán Galán, Alfredo. 2014. Secesión y pertenencia a la unión europea: de Escocia a Cataluña. http://idpbarcelona.net/docs/blog/secesion.pdf.

Garicano, Luis. 2015. El mito económico de la independencia. *EL PAÍS*, September 8. http://elpais.com/elpais/2015/09/07/opinion/1441617574_341810.html.

Gimbernat, Enrique 2018. "Sobre los delitos de rebelión y sedición". *El Mundo*, November 29. https://www.elmundo.es/opinion/2018/11/29/5bfe9f09f-dddff95068b4579.html.

Grau, Mireia. 2011. Self-Government Reforms and Public Support for Spain´s Territorial Model: Changes and Stability. *Revista de Estudios Autonómicos y Federales* (13): 186–214.

Juliá, Santos. 2015. Catalanismos: de la protección a la secesión. *EL PAÍS*, August 29. http://cultura.elpais.com/cultura/2015/08/27/babelia/1440676636_155219.html?rel=lom.

Junqueras, Oriol. 2017. *Catalonia Will Not Retreat*. https://www.nytimes.com/2017/11/01/opinion/catalonia-independence-spain.html.

Keating, Michael. 2012. Rethinking Sovereignty. Independence-Lite, Devolution-Max and National Accommodation. *Revista de Estudios Autonómicos y Federales* (16): 9–29.

Nicolaïdis, Kalypso. 2017. Catalonia and the Theatres of Recognition. https://www.opendemocracy.net/can-europe-make-it/kalypso-nicola-dis/catalonia-and-theaters-of-recognition.

Nieto, Adán. 2018a. Reconocimiento mutuo, orden público e identidad nacional: la doble incriminación como ejemplo. Al margen del caso Puigdemont. https://www.penalecontemporaneo.it/d/6195-reconocimiento-mutuo-orden-pblico-e-identidad-nacional-la-doble-incriminacin-como-ejemplo.

Nieto, Adán. 2018b. The Foundations of Mutual Recognition and the Meaning of Dual Criminality. *European Criminal Law Review* 8 (2): 160–166.

Page, Rob. 2014. *Debate on Possible Independence of Catalonia: Key Issues*. House of Commons Briefing Papers SN06933. http://researchbriefings.parliament.uk/ResearchBriefing/Summary/SN06933.

Plaza, Carmen. 2018. Catalonia's Secession Process at the Constitutional Court: A Never-Ending Story? *European Public Law* 24 (3): 373–392.

Presno Linera, Miguel A. 2015. Law and Disagreement: el 'caso de Cataluña en España'. *Diritto Pubblico* (1): 63–84.

Ridao, Joan. 2018. La aplicación del artículo 155 de la Constitución a Cataluña: Un examen de su dudosa constitucionalidad. *Revista Vasca de Administración Pública* (111): 169–203.

Robinson, Andy. 2014. Will Catalonia Secede from Spain? *The Nation*, October 21. http://www.thenation.com/article/will-catalonia-secede-spain/.

Sarmiento, Daniel. 2018. The Strange (German) Case of Mr. Puigdemont's European Arrest Warrant. https://verfassungsblog.de/the-strange-german-case-of-mr-puigdemonts-european-arrest-warrant/.

CHAPTER 2

Constitutional and Comparative Analysis of the Catalan Secessionist Process

Abstract The chapter analyzes the constitutional framework in which the Catalan secessionist process has developed. It starts by focusing on international law, particularly on the right to self-determination of peoples as established in the UN treaties and case law, and on the so-called remedial secession, and later sums up the two main foreign experiences of secessionism (Québec and Scotland), as well as two relatively minor cases in Bavaria and in Veneto, highlighting the similarities and the differences in respect to Spain and Catalonia. The barring by the Spanish Constitutional Court in 2014 of the "right to decide" and of any kind of referendum on independence is also discussed. The chapter ends with an assessment of the role the EU has played in the secessionist process, particularly of the issue of whether an independent Catalonia would automatically remain in the EU (applying the so called "internal enlargement"), or rather would leave it, and also of the position of relative neutrality adopted by the Commission.

Keywords Right to self-determination · Remedial secession · Referendum · EU · Canada–Québec · UK Scotland · Constitutional Court · Secessionist process · European Commission · Internal enlargement

© The Author(s) 2019
M. Beltrán de Felipe, *Myths and Realities of Secessionisms*,
https://doi.org/10.1007/978-3-030-11632-3_2

1   SECESSION UNDER INTERNATIONAL LAW: SELF-DETERMINATION AND THE SO CALLED "REMEDIAL SECESSION"

The principle of self-determination of peoples, interpreted as a right or entitlement, has been—sometimes not openly or expressly—the basis of the Catalan claims for holding a referendum on independence, and for seceding from Spain. It is more or less generally agreed that self-determination aimed at a territory obtaining independence from the state it is part of has its roots in a report by the League of Nations in 1921 regarding the secession of the Aland islands from Finland.[1] Only in the post-WWII era, and with the precedent of the Atlantic Charter (1941), self-determination was laid into treaties: see article 55 of the UN Charter 1945 (which calls for the respect of the principles "*of equal rights and self-determination of peoples*"), see also UN Declaration on the Granting of Independence to Colonial Countries and Peoples (Resolution 1514 [XV] of December 14, 1960), and later articles 1.1 of both the ICESCR and the ICCPR: "*All peoples have the right of self-determination. By virtue of that right they freely determine their political status and freely pursue their economic, social and cultural development*".

Despite of these declarations of self-determination as a right of the peoples or of the territories, only an extremely small number of countries allow unilateral secession. Only Liechtenstein (1921 constitution), Nevis and St. Christopher (1983 constitution) and Ethiopia (1994 constitution) seem to permit it: see a comparative overview in Sáiz Arnáiz (2006–2007) and in Martinico (2018: 10–13).

In any event, the UN practice and case law the main field of self-determination has been decolonization (in which it started to be construed as a "right"), and therefore could not be applied to Catalonia. Ultimately, as Shikova puts it (2016: 238), outside of the context of decolonization international law has not supported claims for secession. Certainly, there exist some controversy regarding situations such as indigenous peoples and internal self-determination. But the fact is that international law has not recognized to minorities living within a state the right to break away based on the principle, or on the right,

---

[1] Report of the Commission of Rapporteurs, League of Nations Council, Doc B7 21/68/106, 1921: see https://www.ilsa.org/jessup/jessup10/basicmats/aaland2.pdf.

to self-determination. Probably for that reason, in the last two or three decades (mainly, after the fall of the soviet regime) a somewhat different concept was fostered: the concept of "remedial secession" was created and developed by some scholars such as Allen Buchanan in the 1990s, as an alternative or an extension to self-determination.

Would this scholarly-created theory be applicable to Catalonia? I say "scholarly-created" because, as Vidmar explains (2010: 42), there is no state practice at all, that is, remedial secession has never been put into practice (Bangladesh, the Soviet Union, Yugoslavia and Kosovo do not clearly fit into the theory). So would Catalan people have under international law a *right* to decide its own future and to exercise it by seceding from Spain? Apparently, the answer is no. Catalonia would not fit in the criteria or requisites of remedial secession, which basically consist in: (a) a situation of oppression, grievance of injustice suffered by its people in terms of large-scale violations of basic human rights (Cassese speaks of gross breaches of fundamental rights: quoted by Vidmar 2010: 51); (b) unjust taking of a legitimate state's territory; and (c) persistent violation of an intrastate autonomy or self-government agreement. Milanovic (2017) sums up the idea by arguing that even if an entitlement to the so-called remedial secession could be found in modern international law (and he believes it is not the case), Catalonia is historically, politically and above all factually very far from the specific situations in which such right might apply—see a same argument in Shikova (2016). Other authors (Miller, Nielsen) add two factors: there has to be a determined "cultural group" differentiated from the rest of the country which would have suffered the injustice (this focus on the concept of "nation", as encompassing the "cultural group", has been suggested as providing a theoretical, legal solution to the old issue of the "nations without a state"); and also the inexistence of a possible peaceful solution within the state. At any event, the remedial secession theory seems to be little more than a theory—in the sense that it does not have a reflect on international treaties and has not been fully applied. Vidmar (2010: 51) shows that not a single non-colonial new state created since 1950 serves as an undisputed example or remedial secession. Besides, the theory has also been subject to strong criticisms—see Mueller (2012: 293).

So self-determination, as conceived in international law, would not apply to the Catalan problem, nor would the more flexible theory of remedial secession. This would explain why Catalan secessionists have not clearly invoked any of them as a legal basis for obtaining independence from Spain, and instead they drew upon the "right to decide". They mentioned the Canadian Clarity Act 2000 and, in some occasions, also the Kosovo precedent. But neither of both provides Catalan secessionists a firm ground in which affirm the "right to decide", whatever it means, or the right to secede from Spain: for Québec, see Sect. 2.1 of this chapter, and regarding Kosovo, it seems to be the only case in which a unilateral declaration of independence from Serbia (proclaimed on February 17th 2008) has been accepted by international law.[2] It was a controversial decision, adopted by a 10-4 vote, and the Court expressly stated it would not be used as a precedent for other situations—although in the following years some other countries and territories invoked it for recognizing a few unilateral secessions.

In any case, the ICJ's ruling on Kosovo does not seem to be applicable to Catalonia. After the Balkans war and the humanitarian crisis, Kosovo was not under Serbian domination anymore but under an international administration and supervision, and later under the "Provisional Institutions of Self-Government" established by a "Constitutional Framework" issued by the UN. So when it declared itself independent, Kosovo had already broken ties with Serbia, thus Serbian legality was not applicable anymore. As a consequence, the ICJ could not find the unilateral declaration of 2008 contrary to a constitutional order (the Serbian constitution) which was not in force, nor contrary to the Kosovar provisional constitutional order (which did not establish what would happen when power would be returned to Kosovar elected authorities), nor contrary to international law given the violence and injustice caused by Serbia to the Kosovar people. See a critical comment on the ICJ Opinion in Kassoti (2016: 234). At any event, it is very clear that Catalonia is in a completely different situation, because its historical context is by no means comparable to Kosovo, for in Catalonia there has been no war or abuse caused by the state it belongs to, there has been no international administration, and there has been a clear infringement of national constitutional order.

The question of whether there would also be an infringement of international law is also quite clear. Catalan unilateral declaration of independence broke no international law rule, nor found legal basis in any

---

[2] See the Advisory Opinion of the ICJ of 22 July 2010, Accordance with International Law of the Unilateral Declaration of Independence in Respect of Kosovo, available at http://www.icj-cij.org/files/case-related/141/141-20100722-ADV-01-00-EN.pdf.

international rule. But the inexistence of a right to unilateral secession does not mean that such secession is per se illegal (see Vidmar 2010: 41). International law is neutral in respect of secession, and its consequences—mainly, recognition by other States—are of a political kind, and are regulated internationally and not by domestic law. Both aspects are important: international law has to do mainly with statehood, so as far as it is concerned, it is not per se affected by secessionist tensions and can be considered, in general terms, neutral when faced with unilateral declarations of independence such as the one in Catalonia, or as the one in the Italian Padania in 1997 (see Sect. 3.2 of this chapter). Only in very exceptional situations (mainly, decolonisation) can secessions be admitted as a right, Kosovo being one of the latter. Of course, the political aspect is the key issue, because secession ultimately depends on sheer political assessments and considerations through which states decide whether or not they would grant recognition to the new state (Vidmar 2017). And no legal rule, at international, regional or national level regulates how and when this recognition should take place. As Mueller puts it (2012: 315), the unwillingness of the international community to increase cooperation regarding secessionisms movements is a political reason that constitutes the main hurdle to the recognition of a remedial right. The recent case of Crimea, and before that Kurdistan, would demonstrate the clear predominance of politics in the attitude of the international community towards secession.

The only aspect in which Catalan secessionists might see their claims backed by the ICJ Advisory Opinion is the following: the Court—although in an obiter dictum and not as a rationale for the decision—referred to the right of self-determination as jus cogens and as a right of all peoples, apparently not only of those in a colonial context.

It can fairly be concluded that international law gives no "right" to the Catalan government to secede from Spain. As Vidmar (2017) clearly states, in the Catalan conflict there exists no positive entitlement to independence, because secessionists do not have a legal basis, argument or procedure to support their claim to change the territorial status quo. The right to self-determination does not apply, as construed by the UN, nor does the more pro-secession theories of "remedial secession" (which in any case are not unanimously accepted as part of international law). And the two main concrete international precedents (Québec, which I will address immediately, and Kosovo), as interpreted by the Supreme Court of Canada and by the ECJ, are far from supporting Catalan's claims.

Probably this explains that Catalan secessionists leaders (and Scottish leaders as well) did not invoke seriously any of this rules or judgements, and instead they adduce the "right to decide".

2   A First Comparative Approach: The Main Foreign Precedents of a Referendum on Independence

The foreign experiences of Scotland and Québec are constantly invoked by Catalan secessionists, because in both cases secessionist aspirations were channeled through a referendum (twice in Québec). The fact that independence lost in the three referenda does not seem to be a problem for Catalan secessionists—probably because they believe that by the time a hypothetical referendum would be called in Catalonia, a majority of Catalans would support independence. Let's see how the comparison between Catalonia and Québec and Scotland has been built.

2.1   Canada, Québec and the Clarity Act 2000

Canada is the most well-known example of an occidental democracy which has dealt with a secessionist problem and has channeled it through constitutional rules. Since the separatist movement began in Québec in the 1960s, there have been two referenda (both of them only in the Province of Québec, not at national level). In the first referendum on independence, in May 1980, the separatists gained 40% of the votes. In the October 1995 referendum, Québec's vote in favor of separation had increased to just over 49%. This led the Canadian government, in September 1996, to ask the Supreme Court for an advisory opinion on several aspects of Québec secession. Such opinions are called references, and while not binding from a strictly legal standpoint, they are in practical terms binding because of the moral and legal authority of the Court. The Court, in *Reference re Secession of Québec [1998], 2 SCR 217*, issued in August 1998,[3] established a theoretical and constitutional framework which was later taken into a law by the federal parliament, the so called Clarity Act 2000. *An Act to give effect to the requirement for clarity as set out in the opinion of the Supreme Court of Canada in the Québec Secession Reference (S.C. 2000, c. 26).*[4]

---

[3] See https://scc-csc.lexum.com/scc-csc/scc-csc/en/item/1643/index.do.
[4] See http://laws-lois.justice.gc.ca/eng/acts/c-31.8/page-1.html.

The Reference is considered the most important contemporary attempt to establish a legal framework for non-colonial secessions, and was almost unanimously praised. Its basis is that unilateral secession is not viable (for self-determination does not apply, as established in international law and in Canadian constitutional law):

> The secession of Québec from Canada cannot be accomplished unilaterally by the National Assembly, the legislature or government of Québec, that is to say, without principled negotiations, and be considered a lawful act. Any attempt to effect the secession of a province from Canada must be undertaken pursuant to the Constitution of Canada, or else violate the Canadian legal order. (paragraph 104)

Therefore, some process has to be created ex novo to channel the aspiration to secession. This process was suggested in the Reference and was later incorporated in the Clarity Act, which laid down the rules and conditions for a secessionist process in Québec or in any other Province. Its basis, as was just mentioned, is that there is no right to unilateral secession in international law except for colonies and oppressed peoples, which does not apply to Québec. And the content of the process is the following: any future referendum must have the previous approval of the federal House of Commons, must have a clear majority, and must be based on an unambiguous question. If the outcome shows a clear majority for secession, then negotiations will start between the Canadian government and the Provincial government in order to establish the terms of a possible separation agreement. This agreement would be equivalent to a constitutional amendment, and the fact that secession prevailed in the referendum does not mean that the agreement is necessarily reached. So the rules are:

a. previous agreement between the Federation and the territory regarding the referendum itself;
b. clear question (contrary to the question in the previous referendum held in Québec, in 1995, in which the question was: "*Do you agree that Québec should become sovereign, after having made a formal offer to Canada for a new economic and political partnership, within the scope of the Bill respecting the future of Québec and of the agreement signed on 12 June 1995?*")—which should also be agreed;
c. majority vote (50-plus-one is not sufficient); and
d. negotiations should start in order to determine the conditions of the constitutional amendment and of the secession.

In other words: a successful referendum on independence would not create a right or entitlement to independence, but would only trigger a process of democratic deliberation and negotiations. In those negotiations secessionists do not have, strictly speaking, a right to obtain independence but do have credit in order, at least, to be recognized as carriers of a democratic mandate and entitled to a fair negotiation characteristic of the ordinary constitutional amendment process. According to the Court's reference, "*A clear majority vote in Québec on a clear question in favor of secession would confer democratic legitimacy on the secession initiative which all of the other participants in Confederation would have to recognize*" (paragraph 150).

Given that a unilateral or de facto secession is not viable, a constitutional amendment is needed to divide Canada and to validly create the hypothetical new state of Québec. This amendment would happen if secession prevails by a clear majority in a referendum with a clear question and if, as a result, the process of negotiations between Ottawa and Québec ends in an independence agreement. Only after this agreement, tantamount to a constitutional amendment, could a province leave the Canadian state. "*The secession of a province from Canada must be considered, in legal terms, to require an amendment to the Constitution, which perforce requires negotiation*" (paragraph 84 of the reference) "*within the existing constitutional framework*" (paragraph 149). These elements are undisputed, and it is also undisputed—or it should be—that a secessionist victory in the referendum does not mean immediate secession.

However, many other aspects remain unclear: what percentage constitutes a "clear" majority? Does the "clear" majority include not only the votes for secession but also the turnout? How "clear" needs to be the question posed? Who—and when—takes both decisions? How binding is the mandate to negotiate?—that is: once negotiations have started, what would be the margin for the National Government to deny the specific aspirations of the Québec government about the terms of the secession?

As I just said, what should be also clear is that a hypothetical victory of secession the referendum does not mean the territory abandons Canada immediately. This is an important point, which as I will mention later has been overlooked by Catalan secessionists: legally speaking the referendum is not for leaving the country but to initiate negotiations to leave the country. This should also be included in the "clarity" demanded by the law. In these negotiations the Canadian government would be obliged to negotiate in good faith, but not to grant every demand made by provincial separatists. The democratic vote, with a strong, clear or sufficient majority would have no legal effect or entitlement on its own—the only effect would be to force politically the national government to initiate negotiations, which would not have a predetermined outcome. And Canadian constitutional order, and political actors, could not be indifferent to this democratic expression of the will to leave.

In any case, the opinion of the Court, and the subsequent Clarity Act, are based on the essential premise that unilateral independence—that is: declared by the Québec government without or against the constitution or the national government, even after a referendum—is not an option at all. Because the Clarity Act gave Parliament the power to judge whether the referendum yields a clear majority on a clear question, the national government (a) has to agree to the referendum (before it is held) and to the question, which needs to be "clear" enough; (b) has the right—and the duty—after the referendum to examine the clarity of the hypothetical majority; and above all (c) is bound to initiate talks with secessionists during the period of the hypothetical negotiations of the constitutional amendment the secession would consist in.

All this was reluctantly over time accepted by the Bloc Québécois and the secessionists, despite the fact that they voted against the Clarity Act in the House of Commons, and despite the fact that immediately after it was passed, Québec's parliament responded with the so called Bill 99 (*An Act respecting the exercise of the fundamental rights and prerogatives of the Québec people and the Québec State*).[5] Bill 99 declared that the Québec people alone could determine their own future (that is, the political regime and legal status of the province and its relationship with Canada), that no Parliament or Government could undermine this right and that in the event of a referendum on secession, a majority of 50% plus one votes would be sufficient to declare independence (it also said that only the Québec's parliament would have the power to decide on the wording of the question).

As Sáiz Arnáiz argues (2006–2007: 49), Bill 99 was clearly intended at challenging politically the Clarity Act, and over time was appealed to the Superior Court of Québec, who rendered its judgement in April

---

[5] See http://www.assnat.qc.ca/en/travaux-parlementaires/projets-loi/projet-loi-99-36-1.html.

2018.[6] Surprisingly enough, at least from a strictly legalistic perspective, the judgement did not overrule Bill 99, because it did not confer any right to unilateral secession (and in fact the Bill was carefully drafted and did not explicitly contain the concept nor the words "*unilateral secession*"), and, according to the Court, reaffirmed certain principles of Québec's provincial constitution. Writing for the Court, Justice Claude Dallaire ruled that a hypothetical secession should be channeled through the Clarity Act, and interpreted Bill 99 as a mere political declaration, and not as a ripe piece of law which could provide the legal basis for a unilateral declaration of independence. In other words, the Court did not seem to take very seriously Bill 99, and reminded what was said in the 1998 Reference: that, as I will stress later, a secessionist process is mainly of a political nature, and thus law can only establish a minimal framework, within which there is plenty of space for political expression—and Bill 99 was apparently of this kind.

The fact that unilateral secession is not an option is clearly one of the features that the Catalan secessionists tend to overlook when they mention the precedent of the two Québec referenda (in some statements they misinterpreted the Clarity Act saying that they want to follow the Canadian model because it allows a referendum—which is correct—that gives a right to declare independence—which is not correct). But indeed, because under certain conditions it allows a territory to hold a referendum on independence, the Canadian model gives Catalan secessionists the mirror or the argument they need to claim the "right to decide".

What was the role of constitutional law in this debate? Canada has a constitution which is a mixture of codified acts (the classic written text) and uncodified traditions and conventions. It is made of a group of laws, rules, traditions and practices which structure the way the Canadian political system runs. This group which forms the constitution includes many statutes, orders-in-council, and judicial decisions that interpret these written documents. There exist also informal rules,

---

[6] See the judgement in http://citoyens.soquij.qc.ca/php/decision.php?g-recaptcha-response=03AL4dnxpgHgNEM8tYPVZIq2YOnHbNBHpaArXntVowcYC5mxlwyb5Zvf--w8_TKvYB6EREx3MgnaZTL5Jpt8KO7YCirAHcyjSFklnRZy18upqLOuv97t8-HvCY0Cg CUXUf0k49tFH8wTVDQuvsDaye-oXmUIWhwI9XyD5SeGBzvn4DqCKM9tEvc9CRJn O1g9QFY7TlqXg9iLG219rm_VyRXRRQYZS5KAxGDzHG2HK972hwGx8F1h45VSpSp Cuar6ZdGiT4Cvl7uCOaooj8LjalQjIeTOVHT6AbIsAFbzXcJ3RhPJe_7otSK-Y&ID=4C1 3FAC691EF9203813F4041ACC19CCC.

called constitutional conventions, that regulate how political actors have to behave. The two most important constitutional documents are the Constitution Act (1867), which created Canada and set out the division of powers between the federal and provincial governments, and the Constitution Act (1982). This act created for the first time a set of amending procedures for the Constitution (until then, many changes to the Canadian legal system had to be carried out by the British Parliament). This 1982 document also includes the Charter of Rights and Freedoms.[7] Canada has therefore a constitutional system half way between the non-written constitution of the UK and the ordinary written constitutions of most countries, and contains a specific amendment mechanism, which would be eventually used in the secessionist process. In any case, there is no express "indivisibility" clause such as the one in the Spanish, Italian, Australian, French constitutions, or in the US case law. Mr. Stéphane Dion, one of the main political actors of the Québec issue, argues that the reason why there is no written indivisibility clause is not that Canadians do not cherish or value their national identity, but rather is that *"it is too precious to be based on anything other than the will to live together"* (2013).

This leads to what I believe is a crucial argument. Since the 1995 referendum, the Supreme Court's 1998 Reference and the Clarity Act 2000, relatively few times constitutional arguments have been mentioned. If one takes a look at the debates that took place after the 1995 referendum, and particularly during the parliamentary procedure of the Clarity Act, it is striking that sovereignty, territorial integrity, etc. are scarcely mentioned to solve the Québec secessionist process. As the quote of Mr. Dion reveals, emphasis was put on democratically expressed ideas about belonging, or not to belong, to a community. *Demos* seemed to prevail over written texts or over historical concepts such as "sovereignty" or "nation".

Another aspect in which law is put relatively aside is the majority sufficient to trigger the secession process. In determining what specifically is a "clear" majority and how it is verified, the Supreme Court, and later the Federal Parliament in the Clarity Act, did not want to set a precise figure or threshold. The reason for this is a political one. According to the Reference, *"Only the political actors would have the information and*

---

[7] See the official documents in http://laws-lois.justice.gc.ca/eng/Const/Const_index. html.

expertise to make the appropriate judgment as to the point at which, and the circumstances in which, those ambiguities are resolved one way or another" (paragraph 100) and therefore *"it will be for the political actors to determine what constitutes, 'a clear majority on a clear question' in the circumstances under which a future referendum vote may be taken"* (paragraph 101).

Why did the Federal Parliament follow this advice, instead of setting a specific percentage of voters? As Mr. Dion puts it (2013),

> There is a qualitative dimension to assessing clarity, which begs for a political assessment to be done in full understanding of the actual circumstances. Furthermore, setting any kind of threshold in advance would expose us to the risk of leaving such a serious decision as the choice of a country to the results of a judicial recount or the examination of rejected ballots. That would put us all in a very difficult, even senseless position.

As a result,

> The non-justiciability of political issues that lack a legal component does not deprive the surrounding constitutional framework of its binding status, nor does this mean that constitutional obligations could be breached without incurring serious legal repercussions. Where there are legal rights there are remedies, but as we explained in the Auditor General's case, supra, at p. 90, and New Brunswick Broadcasting, supra, the appropriate recourse in some circumstances lies through the workings of the political process rather than the courts. (Supreme Court Reference, paragraph 102)

This solution sets law aside, and other pre-existing legal rules as well, and leaves the final decision to politics. Furthermore, it will be to the House of Commons, predictably not in favor of secession, to decide whether the majority is "clear", that is, sufficient to trigger the negotiation process. And this decision would be taken after the referendum. The Clarity Act 2000 requires the House to state after the referendum whether *"in the circumstances, there has been a clear expression of a will by a clear majority of the population of that province that the province cease to be part of Canada"*. Not having a precise legal rule about what percentage of votes is a "clear majority", and leaving to one of the parties (the House) the political decision about it poses the risk of eroding the whole secession process—some could say, Québécois for instance, that one of the parties is changing the rules after the game has been played (see Guénette 2016; Taillon 2014).

2.2   The UK, Scotland and the 2014 Referendum

Regarding Scotland, the first secessionist episode was quite similar to what would later happen in Catalonia: a regional draft bill, aimed at calling a referendum on independence. In 2010 the Scottish National Party (SNP) minority government introduced a draft bill in the Scottish Parliament, based on a consultation paper and a road map that would lead to independence.[8] Its main philosophy was the following, according to what then-First Minister Mr. Salmond stated on the foreword of the draft bill:

> This Government believes in the sovereignty of the people of Scotland. We are committed to giving the people the opportunity to express their views in a referendum. More than 10 years on from the establishment of the Scottish Parliament the debate in Scotland is no longer about whether or not the Parliament should take on new responsibilities. The people want our Parliament to be able to do more, so the debate is now about how much more. And it is time the people had their say.[9]

According to the draft bill, the referendum would not consist, technically speaking, in independence, but on two questions: "*first, whether the Scottish Parliament should have more devolved responsibility; second, whether there should be an additional transfer of the power to enable Scotland to become an independent country*".

The victory of the SNP in the 2011 regional elections boosted the secessionist agenda. Scottish leaders said they would hold a referendum on independence in October 2014, notwithstanding the fact that the Scottish government, or the Scottish parliament, do not have legal power for such a referendum. After negotiations, and after a process of consultations, an agreement was reached in October 2012 between the British government (then-Prime Minister Cameron) and the Scottish government (then-First Minister Salmond). In the so-called Edinburgh Agreement of 2012 (*Agreement between the United Kingdom Government and the Scottish Government on a referendum on independence for Scotland*),[10] an independence referendum was called in Scotland,

---

[8]See http://www.gov.scot/resource/doc/303348/0095138.pdf.

[9]See https://www.gov.scot/Publications/2010/02/22120157/2.

[10]See the text in https://www.gov.uk/government/uploads/system/uploads/attachment_data/file/313612/scottish_referendum_agreement.pdf.

without a specific threshold of turnout or of majority. Both governments agreed that the referendum should have a clear legal base, be legislated for by the Scottish Parliament, be conducted so as to command the confidence of parliaments, government and people, and deliver a fair test and decisive expression of the views of people in Scotland and a result that everyone will respect. There was no mention of whether its result would be legally binding or not, or of what would happen later in terms of negotiation between the two governments. The agreement paved the way for a vote in autumn of 2014, with a single Yes/No question on Scotland leaving the UK. From a technical point of view, the British government, which has responsibility over constitutional issues, granted limited powers to the Scottish Parliament to hold the referendum through an Order in Council approved on February 2013.

In the explanations presented by Mr. Cameron after the agreement there was no reference to sovereignty, or to the constitution. See, for example, this statement: after laying out the question why having a referendum, he responded that

> I felt, as the prime minister of the UK, I had a choice. I could either say to Scots 'well you can't have your referendum, it is for us to decide whether you should have one.' I think that would have led to an almighty and disastrous battle [between Westminster and Edinburgh]. So I did what I thought was the right thing, which was to say 'you voted for a party that wants independence, you should have a referendum that is legal, that is decisive and that is fair'.[11]

As Tierney (2013) has pointed out, in the Scottish independence debate there was almost no reference to law, or to the constitution. As far as I know, practically every idea or argument (in favor or against independence) was expressed in terms of history, tradition, economy, or "the good or the bad for the country", instead of in terms of a juridical rule. That is, the core of the debate revolved around politics and not around law. Of course this has to do with the fact that the UK has no written constitution: according to the traditional theory, the consensus with respect to some core collective values and principles makes it unnecessary to have a written constitutional document. In that case, this means that when

---

[11] See https://www.theguardian.com/politics/2014/may/08/david-cameron-defends-decision-scottish-independence-referendum. Courtesy of Guardian News & Media Ltd.

Mr. Cameron agreed to hold the referendum he was backed by an implicit constitutional consensus, and only Parliament could have prohibited him to do so. Thus, there was no preexisting legal framework that could govern the negotiations on the referendum, or in general on a hypothetical secession process. This seems to be the key explanation of the Scottish issue: there was political margin for the Government to decide whether or not to hold a referendum and to establish its conditions, rules and consequences. Therefore, then-Prime Minister Cameron was almost free, from a constitutional standpoint, to reach an agreement with the Scottish authorities in order to hold the referendum of September 2014.

2.3   Can Québec and Scotland Be Considered Valid Precedents for Catalan Authorities' Attempt to Hold a Referendum on Independence?

Understandably enough, Catalan secessionists took the Canadian and British referenda as models and as precedents to invoke in their struggle to hold a referendum. Their argument was not a technical, constitutional one but it was political, because based on "democracy". What I mean is that from a strictly legal and constitutional standpoint it was quite clear that secession was contrary to the Spanish constitution, and so was the bid for a referendum on independence (see Sect. 4 of this chapter). In Spain there is no constitutional or political process, or framework, that could channel the "right to decide", the "referendum" (or "consultation"), nor the secession. And, this being the key of the constitutional problem, authorizing a referendum on independence that would be held only in Catalonia would be considered contrary to the Constitution.

The main difference between Canada and the UK, on the one hand, and Spain, on the other, is that the former have non written or relatively flexible constitutions, which at any event do not define the nation or the country as "one and indivisible" and do not speak in a legal context of national sovereignty of the nation's people. By contrast, Spain's constitution expressly states that the nation is indivisible and that sovereignty lies on the people—on the whole people of Spain. The other relevant difference is the meaning of the word "nation". In the UK it is assumed that it is composed of nations, and apparently this has never been a problem, whereas Spain has a very troublesome relationship with the idea of nation, and with the word itself—it has been the subject of enormous political controversy and even of violence.

As I will explain later, article 2 of the constitution, which establishes "*the indissoluble unity of the Spanish Nation*" and makes this nation the only sovereign entity (article 1.2 of the constitution), has been quite unanimously interpreted as requiring that the decision to hold a referendum can only be validly adopted by the national authorities (and not by Catalan parliament), that the hypothetical referendum should take place at national level (and not just in Catalonia), and at any event within the existing constitutional order (which forbids unilateral secession). This means that under the existing Spanish constitution, the national government, or the national parliament, cannot validly bargain with any territory about a regional referendum. It would be contrary to the constitution to authorize any kind of regional referendum on independence. Then-Prime Minister Cameron was almost free, from a legal and constitutional standpoint, to reach an agreement with the Scottish authorities in order to hold the referendum of September 2014, but, according to the Constitutional Court's case law, the Spanish Prime Minister cannot validly authorize a regional referendum on independence because this would be against the constitution.

However, the main difference between the Canadian and Scottish process, on the one hand, and the Catalan process, on the other, is that in Canada and Scotland it was a "constitutional process", in the sense of governed by constitutional rules (and therefore accepted by all parties), whereas the Catalan process was lacking these essential rules (Fossas 2014b, quoting Keating). In that sense, Fossas (2014b) has made it clear that Scotland, Québec and Catalonia are very different situations, from a historical, social and, above all, constitutional point of view. Despite this, Catalan leaders have in many occasions appealed to the precedents of Québec and Scotland: "real democracies" such as Canada and the UK allow people to express themselves, but they claim Spain is undemocratic because it blocks the referendum. In any case, and apart from the "democratic" issue I will address in Chapter 3, Sect. 4, the fact that the Catalan secessionist process has not a constitutional path, and therefore is against the existing law, or contrary to the constitution, is a major differential fact that should not be overlooked.

Regardless of these reflections, the Canadian solution (the Clarity Act) does not apply to the present situation in Catalonia

a. because it lays down the principle that secession has to be agreed and thus it excludes unilateral secession (and this precisely is what Catalan leaders did on September 27th 2017);
b. because it establishes a procedure based upon a minimum agreement between the secessionist territory and the national government (which has not been the case: there has been no procedure at all);
c. because it requires a "clear majority" of citizens pro secession, which again has not been the case in Catalonia; and above all,
d. because a hypothetical victory of secession in the referendum, and by a "clear majority", would not entitle to independence but rather to a process of negotiations with national authorities aimed at establishing the terms of an eventual independence. Secessionists have constantly overlooked this aspect.

In any case, it is important to keep in mind that neither in ordinary elections nor in the two referenda of 2014 and 2017 a "clear majority" was reached. Only in the 2010 Catalan elections secessionist parties got more than 50% of the votes, and the two referenda (the "consultation" of 2014 and the referendum of 2017 banned by the national government) did not meet the ordinary electoral standards and therefore should not be considered as a valid expression of a majority (although they sent a powerful message to the national government and to the rest of the world). In brief, as Fossas (2014b) and Romero Caro (2017) have shown, secessionists misinterpreted (and mythologised) the foreign precedents, particularly the Clarity Act.

3   A Second Comparative Approach: Two Recent Attempts of Referenda on Independence in Europe Blocked by Constitutional Courts

Apart from Québec and Scotland, in the recent years in Europe there have been three different secessionist movements which have been dealt with by the Constitutional Courts: in Catalonia, in Veneto and in Bavaria. Of course, in the three cases circumstances are very different, but nevertheless it can be worth mentioning the constitutional background and how the Courts responded to the secessionist claims.

3.1   Germany and Bavaria

Although the 1949 German Basic Law creates a homogenous, symmetrical federal system, with equal powers given to all the *Länder*, Bavaria has a somewhat particular position in the German Republic because of its geographical dimension, its traditions (it is a majoritarian Roman Catholic zone) and also because of its political and economic power and influence. For instance, the German main center-right party— CDU—technically does not exist in Bavaria, its position being occupied by its twin party, the CSU, with some independence towards the CDU, with a strong regionalist culture and in power in Bavaria since 1946 (except from 1954 to 1957). Most "states" are called *Länder*, but Bavaria (with Saxonia and Turingia) is a *Freistaat* (a free state, meaning "republic"). Part of its population and its political elites have a perception of being different—probably superior, indeed—to the rest of the country. In fact, Bavaria was the last *Land* to join the Federation in 1949, and only in a second vote by its Assembly (the first vote had overwhelmingly rejected the Basic Law). Despite of these circumstances there has been historically no serious secessionist movement, but in the last ten years approximately the Bavarian secession has gained some support and influence (according to polls, the percentage of Bavarians in favor of independence would be around 20–25%: see Nagel 2017). Nevertheless, the secessionist party (*Bayernpartei*) has never received more than 2.1% of popular vote in the regional elections. In the October 14th 2018 elections it got 231.930 votes, so 1.7%, and no seats in the *Landtag*, with a loss of 10% in respect to the previous regional elections of 2013.

The most recent episode of secessionism was a summary decision (not a complete judgment) of the German Federal Constitutional Court of 16th December 2016 that did not accept for consideration an appeal from some Bavarian citizens which wanted to initiate an independence process by holding a referendum—and their claim had been rejected both by national and by Bavarian authorities. The Second Chamber of the Court responded briefly that

> The constitutional complaint is not admitted for decision. In the Federal Republic of Germany, as a national state based on the constitutional power of the German people, States and Länder are not 'masters of the Basic Law'. There is no room under the Basic Law for secessionist

aspirations of individual States. These aspirations violate the constitutional order.[12]

The main argument was that member states, although co-holders of sovereignty (a word which by the way is not mentioned in the 1949 Basic Law), do not have the right and the capacity to secede. They are not the "masters or owners—*Herren*—of the constitution", a power which belongs only to the German people, and therefore an independence referendum violates the constitution if held only in one of the member states. The only constitutional mention of "unity" (and of "self-determination"—not of "sovereignty") is in the Preamble of the 1949 Basic Law (as amended):

> Conscious of their responsibility before God and man, inspired by the determination to promote world peace as an equal partner in a united Europe, the German people, in the exercise of their constituent power, have adopted this Basic Law. Germans in the Länder of Baden-Württemberg, Bavaria, Berlin, Brandenburg, Bremen, Hamburg, Hesse, Lower Saxony, Mecklenburg-Western Pomerania, North Rhine-Westphalia, Rhineland-Palatinate, Saarland, Saxony, Saxony-Anhalt, Schleswig-Holstein and Thuringia have achieved the unity and freedom of Germany in free self-determination. This Basic Law thus applies to the entire German people.

So, despite of the fact that the territories have freely decided to adhere to the Federation (in reality to create it), the resulting political entity is a unitarian one and, above all, the political subject is the German people as a whole—and not the *Länder*. This means that a single territory cannot decide on a matter that clearly affects the constitutional order, because only the German people, as the depositary of the sovereignty (*rectius*: the constituent power), is entitled to decide about the whole nation and its *demos*. As we will see later, this argument is very similar to the response the Spanish Constitutional Court gave to Catalonia's demands for a referendum.

3.2   Italy and Veneto

In Italy there is a quite openly secessionist party, the *Lega Padana* (the Padanian league), a coalition of parties born in the 1980s with strong

---

[12]See the decision (in German) in http://www.bundesverfassungsgericht.de/SharedDocs/Entscheidungen/DE/2016/12/rk20161216_2bvr034916.html.

support in Piedmont, Veneto and Lombardy, that is, the north of Italy. In 1996 the *Lega*, already integrated into the *Lega Nord* (the North league) declared the independence of Padania, Padania being the north part of Italy more or less equivalent to the river Po valley—although the *Lega Nord* also includes in the Padania center regions such as Tuscany, Marche and Umbria. Not only: the *Lega* organized a referendum in 1997 (*"Do you want Padania to become an independent and sovereign Republic?"*), in which 98% of the votes were "Yes", and therefore a Government, a capital (Venice) an anthem and a flag were created. All this was merely symbolic, and not taken seriously by almost anyone in Italy, mainly because the *Lega* was not in power and the referendum could not be considered "official". I mean that it had no legal consequences (except for the fact that some local leaders were prosecuted for "attacking the unity of the Nation", but charges were dropped). The declaration of independence and the referendum, albeit symbolic and without legal value, showed the power of the *Lega*, which eventually became the main support of the Berlusconi's governments in the 2000s and won the general elections of 2018.

Other initiatives of the Veneto regional government, more or less secessionist, did have legal impact (see Tega 2015). In 1992 and in 1998—after the symbolic declaration of independence—the Veneto Region, governed by the *Lega*, passed two bills which tried to establish a procedure for a constitutional reform. Pursuant to these regional bills, the "regional electorate" could be entitled to initiate the procedure of constitutional amendments. The purpose of these amendments was not openly obtaining independence from Italy, but independence was implicitly part of the plan. Both bills were nullified by the Constitutional Court (decisions 470/1992 and 496/2000: see Conte 2015; Martinico 2017) using a procedural argument, rather than a "unitarian" principle: constitutional amendments are a matter to be decided at national level (they can only be initiated by the national parliament and, in some cases, ratified by the Italian people). In 2014 secessionism revived, and civic organizations held an on line, "private" referendum on independence, which for obvious legal reasons was not called a referendum but an "informal consultation" to which regional authorities, although not participating, were close and sympathetic.

In the aftermath of this peculiar, informal referendum (in which 89% of the participants voted for independence), the Veneto regional parliament passed two new bills in June 2014. Bill no 16 was based on

the right to self-determination and spoke about the sovereignty of the
Veneto people, and was aimed at organizing a real independence referendum which would repeat the question of 1997. The bill was brought
to the Constitutional Court, who, predictably, nullified it in judgement
118/2015. The argument was quite simple: by promoting a referendum
on secession from Italy, the Veneto assembly was creating a new sovereign body, which is absolutely contrary to the principles of unity and
indivisibility established in article 5 of the constitution. The other bill, no
15, was not about an independence referendum but about a referendum
which asked the population if they want more self-government. It would
consist in five questions regarding mainly taxes, and a final question
about Veneto becoming a "special region" (Italy is an asymmetrical system in which five Regions out of twenty have a "special status"—Veneto
has an "ordinary status"). The Court, in that same judgment 118/2015
nullified most of the content of the bill, but maintained the possibility
of a non-binding referendum on more self-government. Indeed, within
some limits, but inherent to its legislative initiative vis à vis the national
Parliament, any Region is allowed to pose that question under the Italian
constitution (article 116), interpreted as allowing a Region to hold a
preliminary political consultation (Tega 2015: 1151) as to initiating a
process of devolution of certain powers. And precisely this is what happened: an official—albeit non-binding, strictly speaking—referendum
was held on October 22nd 2017 in Veneto (and also in Lombardy),
with a turnout of 57 and a 98% of "Yes" votes for initiating a negotiation process aimed at demanding to the national government the transfer
of new powers to the Region. Although the question of the referendum
was clearly not on independence, it was somewhat showcased by some
Veneto regional leaders as reflecting the will of independence from Italy.

3.3 Are Veneto and Bavaria Comparable to Catalonia?

From a constitutional standpoint, the situation in Germany and Italy
regarding secession is clear, and very similar to Spain because the three
countries define themselves as indivisible. As has been discussed, article
2 of the Spanish constitution expressly states it, article 5 of the Italian
constitution proclaims the Republic as "one and indivisible", and
although the German Basic Law does not expressly contain such a declaration, the Constitutional Court has said many times that States are
co-sovereign but this status does not include the power to leave the

Federation, because States are not the "masters of the constitution". The rationale is the same: a single territory cannot declare itself independent, this decision belonging to the same *demos* which enacted the constitution, that is, the whole nation in the form of constituent power. This also means that a single territory cannot validly hold a referendum on independence.

So if the existing constitutional framework does not allow secession, nor a referendum on secession, then a constitutional reform would theoretically be needed to validly hold it. In their judgments of 2015 and 2016, neither the Italian nor the German Court mentioned this aspect. I mean that they did not address if a hypothetical constitutional amendment could validly allow a regional referendum on independence, and eventually secession of the territory. The German 1949 Basic Law contains the so-called "eternity clause" (article 79.3) which establishes some aspects that cannot be amended, so they remain "eternal".

> Amendments to this Basic Law affecting the division of the Federation into Länder, their participation on principle in the legislative process, or the principles laid down in Articles 1 and 20 shall be inadmissible.

It is controversial among scholars if the unity of the Germany is included or not in article 79.3, and therefore if it would be possible or not to amend the Basic Law in order to expressly admit the *Länder* to secede— or to initiate a referendarian process aimed at seceding from Germany.

Indeed, there exist similarities between Bavaria, Veneto and Catalonia. The social and economic background is similar in Veneto and in Catalonia: both are rich regions, and tax-payers in northern Italy, and in Catalonia (not so much in Bavaria), have long complained that too much of their revenues go to the central Italian government, which then spends them in poorer regions in the south. Veneto (and Lombardy) are two of Italy's richest regions, producing around 10 and 20% of the country's total GDP respectively. They each pay much more money in taxes to Rome than they receive in investment and services. This fiscal imbalance is apparently more real in Italy than in Spain, though. In any case, the nationalistic, identitarian claim is more present in Catalonia than in the north of Italy, but according to some polls the immigration crisis in Italy in 2016 and 2017 would have boosted a xenophobic, identitarian reaction in the north. And actually the *Lega* won the general elections of

March 2018 and Mr. Salvini (its General Secretary) is currently the Vice-President of the Government.

But although Veneto (since 2010) and Lombardy (since 2013) are governed by the *Lega*, as well as Catalonia is governed by secessionist parties, there are substantial differences between the north of Italy and Catalonia. First, polls say that independence has less popular support in Veneto. Second, in Veneto no "consultation", or referendum, were organized by regional authorities against the explicit prohibition of national Government or Courts (the Veneto government abided to the Constitutional Court's judgement of 2015 that declared illegal the referendum on independence they wanted to hold). And third, above all in Veneto there was no insurrection of local Government—in the past the *Lega Padana* was much more pro unilateral independence, but once in power in Veneto, backed to a relatively more moderate position. In sum, the issues and social demands are similar but the attitude of the regional authorities in Catalonia and Veneto has been different (as Tega titles her paper, "*Venice is not Barcelona*"). Catalonia, in several occasions, has openly defied national government and the Constitutional Court, and has initiated a unilateral secessionist process. By contrast, Veneto (and other parts of the north of Italy) has not followed such an insurrectional path, so Tega (2015: 1154) believes that the Veneto Region, compared to Catalonia, was much more cautious and prudent.

Tega (2015: 1163) writes that public opinion—both at regional and at national level—was substantially indifferent to the bill passed in 2014 by the Veneto Parliament, probably because for many years the *Lega* and its proclamations and referenda were not seen as something serious (it was considered rather a picturesque, eccentric movement). What Tega points out is surely a major difference, and brings up a crucial issue. Does constitutional law (that is, the response of the constitutional courts to secessionist demands) need to take into account if these claims are backed by a significant part of society? López Bofill thinks so, and apparently also Ridao (2018) and Ridao and González (2014: 375)—although in the context of Spain breaching the democratic principles enshrined in EU treaties by not allowing a referendum on secession in Catalonia. López Bofill's argument (2018: 5) is the following: once ruled out the possibility of a referendum, then the popular support for secession can only be expressed in polls and, above all, in free elections to a (regional) parliament. If, as it actually happens, there exists a democratic pressure for secession (or at least for a referendum) freely expressed, and this pressure or will is evident (close to 50% of the votes in the last four elections to the Catalan parliament), then the response of the constitutional system and its interpreters must take into account the existence of this strong popular pressure. Therefore, the original incompatibility between constitutionalism and secession which characterizes liberal democracies could be overcome by allowing a referendum, as the only democratic alternative to deal democratically with the conflict.

According to this view, this sociological, or political aspect (a strong or sufficient popular pressure for secession) should have provoked a different reaction in Spanish authorities (including, of course, the Constitutional Court). The legal response of German or Italian authorities to a referendum on secession would have been correct, given the absence of "strong popular support", but the response by Spanish authorities would have been wrong. López Bofill (2018: 5) writes that denying the possibility of a referendum was a harsh, illiberal reaction—derived by what he calls the hubris of the Spanish institutions on the issue of the indissoluble unity of the nation. This author considers this situation shocking in a liberal democracy, particularly taking into account the scrupulous pacific character of the Catalan movement.

I shall not delve into this matter now (I will make some comments in Chapter 3, Sect. 4). But it is clear that it poses a serious issue, from a theoretical perspective: should constitutional adjudication differ when one of the claims or one of the sides has strong popular support? Should constitutional law lawyers or judges adapt a clearly "No" answer to a referendum, depending on the social or electoral support of the parties, or depending on the magnitude of the criticisms or of the repudiation the judgement would provoke? Bluntly posed, the dilemma is whether a correct, legitimate legal answer on an independence referendum depends, as López Bofill seems to imply, on the popular support for the referendum or for secession. And, subsequently, and similarly to the "clear majority" of the Canadian solution, the key factor would be how "strong" (measured in percentage of the voters) needs to be the popular support in order to make the judgment acceptable or legitimate.

This is not just a scholarly debate. It also raises relevant problems from a purely practical point of view, as I will later mention in chapter three when commenting the existence, or not, in Spain of other constitutional solutions regarding the referendum and secession.

4   THE CONSTITUTIONAL SITUATION IN SPAIN
(ACCORDING TO THE CONSTITUTIONAL COURT)

The first legal issue which appeared was the proclamation of Catalonia as a sovereign entity or nation, entitled to the "right to decide". This right was defined as *"the imprescriptible and inalienable right of Catalonia to self-determination as a democratic expression of its sovereignty as a nation"*, as an instrument for *"the need for Catalonia to make its own way and for the Catalan people to be able to decide their collective future freely and democratically in order to ensure social progress and economic development, to strengthen democracy and to promote their own culture and language"* (Resolution no 742/IX of the Parliament of Catalonia, on the general political orientation of the Government of Catalonia, adopted on September 27th 2012).[13]

This was followed by another resolution, in January 2013. By a 85-41 vote, a resolution was passed *"about sovereignty and about the right of the Catalan people to decide"*.[14] This declaration was based on the principle that the Catalan people is a sovereign subject from a legal and from a political standpoint, and asserts that "Spain" had twice blocked the legitimate aspirations of self-government:

> The impediments and refusals by the institutions of the Spanish State, especially Judgment 31/2010 of the Spanish Constitutional Court, lead to a radical rejection of the democratic evolution of the collective will of the Catalan people within the Spanish State and lay the foundations for a retrogression in self-government, which is very apparent today in the political, jurisdictional, financial, social, cultural and linguistic fields.

Importantly enough, there was a clear shift from the previous positions: up to 2010, the main vindications and demands of nationalists was the recognition of Catalonia as a nation. But starting from 2010, and leading up to the 2012 and 2013 Resolutions, the claim became that Catalonia was a sovereign nation.

[13] Available in English at http://www.parlament.cat/web/documentacio/altres-versions/resolucions-versions.

[14] Available in English at http://www.parlament.cat/web/documentacio/altres-versions/resolucions-versions.

Scholars such as Fossas (2014a: 285, 290–291) and Ferreres (2014: 578) have pointed out that both resolutions seem to be deliberately ambiguous and confusing (Fossas uses at least six times the epithet "*ambiguous*"), for they do not explicitly claim for a secessionist referendum, and for they equate the "right to decide" (whose content and scope are not precisely defined) with the "right to be heard" and, apparently, also with the "right so secede". Probably the reason for this confusion is to deliberately avoid using the idea, and sometimes the word itself, of self-determination (at least in the main secessionist documents), because international law applies it only to decolonization processes (see Sect. 1 of this chapter), and this might have been considered detrimental for the legal legitimacy of the secessionist claims. In any case, Catalan secessionists perhaps overlooked that the "right to decide" could have been exercised in 1978, in the form of constituent power, by overwhelmingly adhering in a referendum to the Spanish constitution. Most importantly, the resolutions passed by Catalan parliament in 2012 and 2013 do not establish nor invoke any kind of constitutional procedure or path which would control the exercise of this right, or would channel the "sovereigntist process". A great number of constitutional law scholars, including Catalan scholars (Tornos 2014; Fossas 2014a; Galán 2013, 2014a, b; Ferreres 2014; Roig 2017) agree that the "right to decide" is legally non-existing, at national or at international level. Its only basis would apparently be somehow linked with natural law, or with the blurred legal theories of the *volksgeist* romanticism, or with the so called "remedial secession"—interpreted in an extremely loose way (see a different thesis, openly sympathetic to secessionism, in Ridao 2014).

In any case, it was quite obvious that Catalan leaders were implying that the "right to decide" they were invoking included the right to unilaterally determine whether to secede from Spain. As was predictable, after the soverigntist Resolutions each side took action immediately. The national government challenged the January 2013 resolution before the Constitutional Court, and the Catalan government started the process in order to implement the "right to decide", announcing a referendum which would take place in Catalonia in November 2014. Aware that only national Government has the power to validly organize such referendum, on January 2014 the Catalan Government officially requested the national parliament to transfer this specific power. The answer was also 100% predictable: the national Parliament turned down the request in a 299-47 vote. The Catalan government now had one more grievance to add to the list, because according to its political discourse, Spain was again illegitimately and undemocratically denying to Catalans the simple, essential right to be heard, or to decide.

In March 2014 the Constitutional Court rendered its judgment (number 42/2014) about the 2013 Resolution (see Ferreres 2014; Fossas 2014a; Plaza 2018; Roig 2017; Ridao 2014; Presno 2015).[15] See other judgements rendered by the Court on other aspects the Catalan secessionist process: number 31 and 32/2015, number 138/2015, number 259/2015, number 51/2017, number 90/2017, number 114/2017 and number 124/2017, most of them regarding a Catalan law on "non refrendarian popular consultations", and the last two regarding the "*disconnection bills*" number 19 and 20/2017, passed on September 6th and 7th 2017, which gave way to the October 1st referendum. See also a relatively critical assessment of these judgments in Roig (2017: 55 ff.), and a much more severe opinion in López Bofill (2018).

Judgement 42/2014 was an important, relatively pondered decision, which quoted the 1998 Canadian reference regarding Québec—see a critical comment in Fossas (2014a), pointing out both its reasoning flaws or what he calls reasoning manoeuvres and the out of context, incorrect quoting of the Reference, which aspect has also been underlined by Romero Caro (2017: E145) The Court invalidated the "principle of sovereignty" that is at the basis of the 2013 resolution and of the secessionist movement. The rationale of the judgment was that articles 1 and 2 of the Constitution are clear on this matter because they state that national sovereignty, and the constituent power, belong to the Spanish people as a whole, not to one of its parts such as Catalonia. Therefore, the nation, as well as the sovereignty in which it lies in, is indivisible, and accordingly Catalans (or any other people within Spain) cannot have a referendum on matters on which all Spaniards are sovereign. Only the nation, the whole Spanish *demos*, as constituent and sovereign power, can validly decide about its territory—and about the constitution. Therefore, under the Spanish 1978 constitution, as well as under the German and the Italian constitutions, Catalan authorities cannot unilaterally call a local referendum of self-determination to decide on its integration in Spain.

---

[15] An English version is available at http://www.tribunalconstitucional.es/es/jurisprudencia/restrad/Paginas/STC42-2014.aspx.

Regarding specifically the "right to decide", the Court considered it a mere "aspiration" and not a piece of ripe or applicable law, in a reasoning somewhat similar to the April 2018 judgement of the Superior Court of Québec regarding Bill 99. Accordingly, the Court upheld the corresponding parts of the resolution, interpreted as expressing a political principle that could be eventually implemented within the constitutional framework and through legally established procedures. Ferreres (2014: 580) writes that it was a solomonic decision, for it did not per se bar the "right to decide", whatever it consists on, but channeled it through hypothetical, eventual constitutional provisions. Ridao (2014: 94) stresses the fact that, in his view, the judgment did not rule out the "right to decide" because it construed it in a non-unconstitutional fashion which could, at least hypothetically, be feasible—but after a constitutional reform.

This last aspect is the key factor, because the Court said in judgment 42/2014 that a constitutional reform was needed in order to legally exercise this right:

> Any approach that intends to change the very grounds of the Spanish constitutional order is acceptable in law, as long as it is not prepared or upheld through an activity that infringes democratic principles, fundamental rights or all other constitutional mandates, and its effective achievement follows the procedures foreseen for constitutional reform, given that these procedures are inexcusable (STC 103/2008, FJ 4) [...] For the foregoing reasons, we hereby conclude that the references made to the "right to decide" in the challenged Resolution, following a constitutional interpretation based on the principles examined above, do not contradict the Constitution and, overall, subject to the exceptions described herein, express a political aspiration that may be upheld in the constitutional order.

This is similar—but only similar—to the Canadian solution: the existing constitutional model does not allow secession nor a referendum (although in Canada the referendum was admitted), and therefore it would be necessary to change it. At any event, this poses the problem of the limits of constitutional reforms. Unlike the aforementioned German constitution (article 79.3), the Spanish Constitution has no "eternity clause", and therefore any of its provisions is subject to revision. In other words, constitutional amendments have no substantial limits, its limits being only procedural. So even the "sovereignty clause" and the "indivisibility clause" (articles 1 and 2 of the constitution) could in theory be amended in order to make it legal for Catalonia, or for other "nationality" or "region", to unilaterally decide about its political ties with Spain or to directly secede from Spain. I will analyze the amendment matter in Chapter 3, Sect. 5.2, but let me say now that I consider this constitutional amendment extremely unlikely.

The Court's ruling, establishing the impossibility of an agreed referendum on secession, is the orthodox, mainstream vision, and almost no one in the national political field considered that the 42/2014 judgment could be partially wrong or that there could exist other possible solutions which might permit some kind of referendum. I will return to this in Chapter 3, Sect. 5.3.

5   THE EUROPEAN QUESTION

One of the many paradoxes, or contradictions, present in the Catalan secessionist process is the role the EU is supposed to play. This same question could also be found in the Scottish process (see Keating 2015), and is still under debate because of the *Brexit*. The motto of one of the vast demonstrations in 2012 was "*Catalonia, a new European state*", clearly implying that, according to Catalan leaders, if Catalonia seceded from Spain it would automatically remain in the EU. This was called by the secessionist leaders and scholars a "domestic or internal enlargement" of the EU, meaning that the part or region of a member state that seceded would not necessarily be considered a foreign state seeking for EU membership, but the situation would rather be interpreted as a result of an internal frontier modification which does not need to trigger the ordinary admission process as laid down in article 49 TUE (see a development of the "internal enlargement" theory in Walker 2015, and mainly in Ridao and González 2014: 384 ff.). According to this view, after a hypothetical secession of Catalonia there would be no "external enlargement", because Catalonia would not be considered a third state: it was a EU territory when it was part of Spain and it would still be EU territory after secession from Spain. Thus, it would automatically remain as a EU member.

What was the attitude of the European Commission towards the Catalan issue? In the spring of 2015 President Juncker's speaker said that Catalonia's issue was an internal constitutional matter, upon which the Commission had no opinion. And pursuant to article 4.2 TEU ("*The Union shall respect the equality of Member States before the Treaties as well as their national identities, inherent in their fundamental structures, polit-ical and constitutional, inclusive of regional and local self-government"*), EU authorities are committed to respect domestic, regional matters of the member states. In 2014 and 2015 EU officials stated that the EU consid-ers important "the different expressions of democracy", but were not more specific. In any case, until September 2015 there was no clear position of the EU and, in particular, there had been no clear support from the EU to the Catalan secessionist process. On the one hand, the EU considered it an internal matter, and did not want to intervene, but on the other hand there were some insinuations that it would appreciate some dialogue or flexibility by both parties—similarly to what had happened in Scotland. In any case, media suggested that there was relief in Brussels after the result of the Scottish referendum in September 2014, and that the Catalan seces-sion process was not welcome. As the September 2015 Catalan elections were closer, the Spanish Government pushed the Commission and obtained a declaration of Mr. Juncker's speaker which expressly stated that an inde-pendent Catalonia would be out of the EU.[16]

Things changed when the unilateral secession process started in late 2016 (that is: when the referendum was unilaterally called by the Catalan government and was declared illegal by the Constitutional Court). The Catalan government wanted to legitimize its position by requiring a mediation or facilitation by the EU, and then-Prime Minister Rajoy demanded, and eventually obtained, a tougher position from the EU. After the 1st October 2017 referendum, the Commission issued a state-ment which openly contradicted the secessionists' "internal enlarge-ment" thesis: *"If a referendum were to be organized in line with the Spanish Constitution it would mean that the territory leaving would find itself outside of the European Union."*[17] Indeed, a small group of mem-bers of the European Parliament criticized police violence against vot-ers—but neither the Commission, or the Counsel, would follow. And Mr. Junker explained why the EU did not want to be involved, meaning that the Commission could not mediate if calls to do so came only from one side—in this case, the Catalan government—and also because this

[16]See http://politica.elpais.com/politica/2015/09/17/actualidad/1442481238_663863.html.

[17]See "Statement on the events in Catalonia" from October 2nd 2017, available at http://europa.eu/rapid/press-release_STATEMENT-17-3626_en.htm.

involvement "*will create a lot more chaos in the EU*". His main point was that "*If Catalonia is to become independent, other people will do the same. I don't like that. I don't like to have a euro in 15 years that will be 100 different states. It is difficult enough with 27 states. With many more states it will be impossible.*"[18] See a similar idea in Weiler (2014b). Interestingly enough, according to this statement, Mr. Junker seemed to assume that Catalonia would remain a EU member and a Eurozone member—or at least would re-join the EU after a short time.

Few weeks after the unilateral declaration of independence of October 27th 2017, then-Catalan President Mr. Puigdemont was prosecuted and flew immediately to Brussels, and he complained angrily against the EU, accusing it not to support democracy and suggesting that when he would be in power again he would call a referendum to know if Catalans want to remain in the EU.[19]

The "internal enlargement" thesis advocated by the secessionist leaders and by some scholars is undoubtedly groundless. First, because the Commission expressly said, in the aforementioned statement of October 2nd 2017, that a seceded Catalonia would leave the EU. The EU position is absolutely clear, and not debatable anymore. Furthermore, the Commission's "Statement on the events in Catalonia" of October 2nd 2017 mentioned an independence process "*in line with the Spanish Constitution*", and this clearly means that a unilateral, illegal process would even less be considered by the EU. Second, because even without the Commission's statement, according to international law and to EU law if hypothetically Catalonia would become an independent state, it would not remain as a member of the EU. EU treaties would not be applicable to this new state. As Galán (2013, 2014a), Weiler (2012, 2014a, b), and partially Closa (2016) have convincingly discussed, if Catalonia, or Scotland, would obtain independence from Spain or from the UK they would automatically leave the EU and in order to re-join they would need to initiate the ordinary enlargement procedure. EU Treaties would no longer apply to a seceded territory, and this new independent state will have to apply for membership, if it is interested. And ultimately, as Closa stresses (2016: 260), new EU membership would

---

[18] See https://www.theguardian.com/world/2017/oct/13/eu-intervention-in-catalonia-would-cause-chaos-juncker-says. Courtesy of Guardian News & Media Ltd.

[19] See the article "Carles Puigdemont calls for Catalonia to leave EU", at https://www.thetimes.co.uk/article/puigdemont-calls-for-catalonia-to-leave-eu-zsfj96ph0.

need to be formalized by means of a new treaty. Indeed, Walker (2015: 7) is right when he argues that international law is relatively fluid on this matter, but in my opinion this does not mean that the "internal enlargement" thesis is correct, for it only reveals the traditional political component of international public law.

So a *Catalexit* would mean leaving the EU, just like Scotland would have left the EU if the 2014 referendum had succeeded and independence would have been negotiated and obtained from the UK. In sum, as Weiler writes (2014b), the so-called "automaticity" is unpersuasive, mainly because citizenship of the Union is based on being nationals of a member state, and if Scotland, or Catalonia, would deliberately become independent, then their people would no longer be nationals of a member state, and this means that EU membership would not be automatic. International public law and EU law are sufficiently clear on this matter, and EU leaders and speakers have stated it in many occasions.

Indeed, the EU's attitude towards Catalan secession is not without flaws. As Walker argues (2015: 10), EU leaders have shown a prudential minimalism added to conservative neutrality, instead of having at least tried to deal with what he calls "the political morality" of the secessionist claims in Scotland and in Catalonia—just as EU leaders do not seem to be doing with immigration. Walker believes that this reveals weakness, instead of strength. Of course, the debate has a moral component, and it might cut both ways. The fact that many (Catalan and Scottish secessionists) would have reclaimed from the EU a more political implication with part of its *demos* does not overshadow that other *demoi* (Spaniards and Britons which seemingly do not want the secession of a part of their country) might deserve at least the same deference. For the EU, opting for secessionist of for unionists would have meant, as Walker suggests, assuming a moral political stand. Indeed, supporting the secessionists bids might have been considered a "democratic" position. But not doing so can be also deemed as founded in moral, arguable reasons. And also founded in a democratic view of the domestic political processes at member state level. What I mean is that I do not think, as Weiler's critics argue (Walker 2015: 7), that considering that if Catalonia (and Scotland) would secede from Spain or from the UK they would not remain in the EU is not a "too stringent" approach. And similarly I believe that the EU not wanting to get involved in the secessionist processes is both constitutionally correct, and probably politically preferable, for the following reasons:

a. it is based on moral, historical principles (for Europe is built on integration, and in yielding sovereignty, instead of in disintegration and in claiming sovereignty);
b. particularly, the non-involvement is at least as "democratic" as Walker's, and others', ideas, for respecting the domestic constitutional identity can fairly be considered a democratic feature of the EU;
c. it is based on the EU treaties (as Closa argues, 2016: 263, unilateral secession, such as Catalan leaders have promoted, is incompatible with fundamental EU principles such as the rule of law and democracy); and
d. it is also based on practical, pragmatic, sound considerations which cannot be disdained.

In sum, in my view the "conservative neutrality" (Walker) of the EU is not unprincipled nor "morally" flawed.

However, as some scholars argue (Ridao and González 2014: 380 ss.; Walker 2015: 15), it is also clear that in case of an independent Catalonia (or Scotland) some temporary arrangement would be found to avoid some chaotic situation (currency, visas, borders, investments and banking, etc.), and that probably the EU would speed up the political decisions in order to readmit seceded, new countries, essentially because they previously belonged to the EU. Actually, some scholars such as Closa (2016: 245 ff.) have carefully drafted a convincing situation model in which independence (and being a third party to the EU) and a temporary agreement regarding the four liberties would be put into practice. Even notable, non pro-secession scholars such as Weiler, which believe that seceded Scotland and Catalonia would leave the EU, acknowledge that they could join it relatively easily: "*On the technical side [Scotland's] accession should be a relatively easy one, since the European legal acquis is part of the political and legal fabric of Scotland. The adjustments necessary will be, for the most part, of a technical nature*" (Weiler 2014a: 507). So a seceded Scotland (or Catalonia) would not remain in the EU: they would leave simultaneously as they would secede from the UK or from Spain, but they could rejoin the EU relatively quickly, and very likely during the accession period they would benefit from a pre-entry status. Of course, in the event of a secession of Catalonia, in order to re-admit it as a new, independence member state, the EU would take into account some key factors such as the reaction of the member states (at least the most important ones), or if the secession had been unilateral or agreed, or if the reaction of the national government had been proportionate, etc. As Ridao and González write (2014: 383), this EU reaction would be based on pragmatism rather than in principles—contrary to the principled, democratic approach these scholars support. Accession to the EU or secession from a member state (and from the EU) are indeed subject to procedures and to legal rules, but as *Brexit* and the interpretation of article 50 TEU are reflecting, politics and bargaining can surely modulate the enforcement of legal norms.

At any event, from a political standpoint, and also from a strictly legal perspective, the Commission or the Council have good reasons not to intervene in secessionist processes—and of course not to support secessionist leaders. Apart from Scotland and Catalonia, they are perfectly aware of some nationalist inclinations in regions such as Flanders, the north of Italy, and perhaps Corsica, and out of the EU, as well in not so peripheral regions like the Balkans or Ukraine. So taking part in the secessionists processes would mean political trouble, and we should keep in mind that the EU is based on the (partial) suppression of sovereignty and the (almost complete) suppression of frontiers. Thus politically, and probably constitutionally, it is not expectable that the EU take a friendly approach to secessionisms—and this stand, in my view, is not immoral nor undemocratic.

The other claim of Catalan secessionists regarding the EU is about human rights and democratic principles and values. In some of the documents published by the Advisory Board for the National Transition of Catalonia (2014) it is stated that if Spain does not allow the referendum on independence, it would breach the democratic principle that animates European Union treaties, and therefore proceedings against Spain could be initiated before the European Commission or before the European Court—or even before the ECHR. Similarly, some scholars affirm that non allowing a referendum (and later using police force against voters and demonstrators on the October 1st referendum, followed by the prosecution and imprisonment of Catalan leaders and by direct rule from October 2017 to May 2018) is contrary to the rule of law, to the democratic principle and to human rights (article 2 TEU): see Ridao and González (2014: 375) and López Bofill (2018). Accordingly, there would be sufficient basis to trigger against Spain the measures and sanctions established in article 7 TEU. In Chapter 3, Sect. 4, I will comment on these opinions, which I consider unfounded, or at least exaggerated.

REFERENCES

Advisory Board for the National Transition. 2014. *The National Transition of Catalonia.* http://presidencia.gencat.cat/web/.content/ambits_actuacio/consells_assessors/catn/informes_publicats/llibre_blanc_angles.pdf (English version).

Closa, Carlos. 2016. Secession from a Member State and EU Membership: The View from the Union. *European Constitutional Law Review* 12 (2): 240–264.

Conte, Francesco. 2015. La Corte costituzionale sui referendum per l'autonomia e l'indipendenza del Veneto. Non c'è due senza tre. Anche se.... *Quaderni Costituzionali* (3): 759–761.

Dion, Stéphane. 2013. Secession and Democracy: A Canadian Perspective. http://www.realinstitutoelcano.org/wps/portal/rielcano_en/contenido?WCM_GLOBAL_CONTEXT=/elcano/elcano_in/zonas_in/europe/stephane-dion-secesion-democracia-secession-democracy-canada.

Ferreres Comella, Victor. 2014. The Spanish Constitutional Court Confronts Catalonia's 'Right to Decide' (Comment on the Judgment 42/2014). *European Constitutional Law Review* 10 (3): 571–590.

Fossas Espadaler, Enric. 2014a. Interpretar la política: Comentario a la STC 42/2014, de 25 de marzo, sobre la declaración de soberanía y el derecho a decidir del pueblo de Cataluña. *Revista Española de Derecho Constitucional* (101): 273–300.

Fossas Espadaler, Enric. 2014b. Secesión: del proceso eufemístico al constitucional. *EL PAÍS*, November 25. http://elpais.com/elpais/2014/11/24/opinion/1416842833_782695.html.

Galán Galán, Alfredo. 2013. Secesión de Estados y pertenencia a la Unión Europea: Cataluña en la encrucijada. *Istituzioni del Federalismo* (1): 95–135.

Galán Galán, Alfredo. 2014a. Secesión y pertenencia a la unión europea: de Escocia a Cataluña. http://idpbarcelona.net/docs/blog/secesion.pdf.

Galán Galán, Alfredo. 2014b. Del derecho a decidir a la independencia: la peculiaridad del proceso secesionista en Cataluña. *Istituzioni del Federalismo* (4): 885–907.

Guénette, Dave. 2016. Initier le processus constituant en contexte plurinational – Étude comparative des pouvoirs catalans et québécois de mettre en branle de la procédure de révision constitutionnelle de leur État. *Revista de Estudios Autonómicos y Federales* (24): 46–79.

Kassoti, Eva. 2016. The Sound of One Hand Clapping: Unilateral Declarations of Independence in International Law. *German Law Journal* 17 (2): 215–236.

Keating, Michael. 2015. The Scottish Independence Referendum and After. *Revista de Estudios Autonómicos y Federales* (21): 73–9.

López Bofill, Héctor. 2018. Hubris, Constitutionalism, and 'The Indissoluble Unity of the Spanish Nation': The Repression of Catalan Secessionist

Referenda in Spanish Constitutional Law. *I.CON. International Journal of Constitutional Law* 17 (forthcoming).

Martinico, Giuseppe. 2017. Identity Conflicts and Secession Before Courts: Three Case Studies. *Revista General de Derecho Público Comparado* (21): 1–30.

Martinico, Giuseppe. 2018. How Can Constitutionalism Deal with Secession in the Age of Populism? The Case of Referendums. *Sant'Anna Legal Studies— STALS Research Paper 5/2018*. http://www.stals.sssup.it/files/martinico%20 5%202018%20stals.pdf.

Milanovic, Marko. 2017. A Footnote on Secession. https://www.ejiltalk.org/ a-footnote-on-secession/.

Mueller, Charlotte. 2012. Secession and Self-Determination—Remedial Right Only Theory Scrutinised. *Polis Journal* 7: 283–321.

Nagel, Klaus-Jürgen. 2017. Bavaria: Another Case of a Right to Decide? https://repositori.upf.edu/handle/10230/28277.

Plaza, Carmen. 2018. Catalonia's Secession Process at the Constitutional Court: A Never-Ending Story? *European Public Law* 24 (3): 373–392.

Presno Linera, Miguel A. 2015. "Law and Disagreement: el 'caso de Cataluña en España'". *Diritto Pubblico* (1): 63–84.

Ridao, Joan. 2014. La juridificación del derecho a decidir en España. *Revista de Derecho Político* (91): 91–136.

Ridao, Joan. 2018. La aplicación del artículo 155 de la Constitución a Cataluña: Un examen de su dudosa constitucionalidad. *Revista Vasca de Administración Pública* (111): 169–203.

Ridao, Joan, and Alfonso González Bondía. 2014. La unión europea ante la eventual creación de nuevos estados surgidos de la secesión de estados miembros. *Revista de Derecho de la Unión Europea* (27): 363–390.

Roig i Molés, Eduard. 2017. The Catalan Sovereignty Process and the Spanish Constitutional Court: An Analysis of Reciprocal Impacts. *Revista Catalana de Dret Públic* (54): 24–61.

Romero Caro, Francisco Javier. 2017. The Spanish Vision of Canada's Clarity Act: From Idealization to Myth. *Perspectives on Federalism* 9 (3): E-133–E-159. http://www.on-federalism.eu/index.php/component/content/article/ 231-essay/273-the-spanish-vision-of-canadas-clarity-act-from-idealization-to-myth.

Sáiz Arnáiz, Alejandro. 2006–2007. Constitución y secesión. *Parlamento y Constitución. Anuario* (10): 33–56.

Shikova, Natalija. 2016. Practicing Internal Self-Determination Vis-a-Vis Vital Quests for Secession. *German Law Journal* 17 (2): 237–264.

Taillon, Patrick. 2014. De la clarté à l'arbitraire: le contrôle de la question et des résultats référendaires par le parlement canadien. *Revista de Estudios Autonómicos y Federales* (20): 13–59.

Tega, Diletta. 2015. Venezia non è Barcellona. Una via italiana per le rivendicazioni di autonomia? *Le Regioni* (5–6): 1141–1155.

Tierney, Stephen. 2013. Legal Issues Surrounding the Referendum on Independence for Scotland. *European Constitutional Law Review* 9 (3): 359–390.

Tornos Mas, Joaquín. 2014. "El problema catalán: una solución razonable". *El Cronista del Estado Social y Democrático de Derecho* (42): 44–53.

Vidmar, Jure. 2010. Remedial Secession in International Law: Theory and (Lack of) Practice. *St Antony's International Review* 6 (1): 37–56.

Vidmar, Jure. 2017. Catalonia: The Way Forward Is Comparative Constitutional Rather Than International Legal Argument. https://www.ejiltalk.org/author/jvidmar/.

Walker, Neil. 2015. *Internal Enlargement in the European Union: Beyond Legalism and Political Expediency*. Edinburgh School of Law Research Paper No. 2015/32; Europa Working Paper No. 2015/05. Available at SSRN: https://ssrn.com/abstract=2676025 and in http://dx.doi.org/10.2139/ssrn.2676025 (later in Carlos Closa (ed.). 2017. *Secession from a Member State and Withdrawal from the European Union: Troubled Membership*, 32–47. Cambridge: Cambridge University Press).

Weiler, Joseph H.H. 2012. Editorial: Catalonian Independence and the European Union. *The European Journal of International Law* 23 (4): 910–912.

Weiler, Joseph H.H. 2014a. Editorial: Scottish Independence and the European Union. *I.CON. International Journal of Constitutional Law* 12 (3): 507–510.

Weiler, Joseph H.H. 2014b. Scotland and the EU: A Comment. *UK Constitutional Law Association*. https://ukconstitutionallaw.org/2014/09/10/debate-j-h-h-weiler-scotland-and-the-eu-a-comment/.

CHAPTER 3

Paradoxes, Mistakes, and Possible Steps Towards an Appeased Solution

Abstract This chapter provides an overview of the political situation provoked by the Catalan secessionist challenge, and tries to find an answer to the question of whether there exists a way out of the conflict which would fit in the Spanish constitution. After highlighting some paradoxes present in the secessionist process, focus is brought to a critical assessment of the policies and attitudes of the national government and of Catalan secessionists. The mistakes and misinterpretations which both sides committed are critically discussed, particularly regarding the democratic principle—which, according to both parties, is at the heart of their claims, and in any case is on their side. The core of the chapter is an analysis of a possible solution of the conflict, through a referendum (which according to most scholars would require first a constitutional amendment), through a federalist constitutional reform, or through the definition of Spain as a "nation of nations".

Keywords Democracy · Dialogue · Nationalism · Plurinational Spain · Referendum · Constitutional amendment · Police intervention · Secessionist process · Constitutional Court · Federalism, constituent power · Sovereignty · National government

© The Author(s) 2019   77
M. Beltrán de Felipe, *Myths and Realities of Secessionisms*,
https://doi.org/10.1007/978-3-030-11632-3_3

1   SOME PARADOXES

In the Catalan secessionist process I find it easy to perceive a few paradoxes and striking aspects. First, it is striking that a regional Parliament
(and Government) has led, in an occidental, democratic, decentralized and law abiding nation such as Spain, an insurrection against the
national government. As far as I know, this is unprecedented. Second,
it is striking that this secessionist movement sets off from a situation
of advanced self-government (elected legislature, powers in most areas
of government, police, taxes, etc.) which after the 2006 "*Estatuto*" is
similar to federated States (except regarding the judiciary). At General
Franco's death in 1975 probably most Catalans could not have envisaged
that such political power and self-government would ever be granted to
Catalonia. This is why many might consider unexpected, and not easy
to understand, that a relatively high percentage of Catalans judge this
situation unsatisfactory from a self-government point of view—in reality
from an identitarian sentiment. According to the official polling agency
of the Catalan Government, in mid-2018 62.3% of Catalans believe that
Catalonia has an insufficient level of self-government.[1] This dissatisfaction can be considered a paradox, or at least a striking circumstance.

Third, it is striking that the goal of full independence, as a Catalan
Republic, albeit being clearly impossible to obtain, at least in the very
brief deadlines set by Catalan authorities in their road map, was nevertheless pushed by the secessionist leaders. Fourth, it is striking that
independence was planned to be obtained unilaterally and unlawfully,
that is, without or against the will of the national authorities and in a
straight breach of the constitution (and also of some essential democratic rules, for the two "disconnection bills" of September 6th and 7th
2017 which triggered the secessionist process were passed by the Catalan
parliament using a procedure which clearly infringed the rights of the
opposition). Fifth, it is striking that the secessionist process was at least
partially based on inaccurate or distorted information and data spread by
Catalan leaders. For example, they argued that an independent Catalonia
would remain in the EU, that corporations would not leave Catalonia if
it declared independence, that some other States would recognize and

---

[1] See http://upceo.ceo.gencat.cat/wsceop/6748/Resumen%20en%20Espa%C3%B1ol%
20-901.pdf.

independent Catalonia, that Spain was a totalitarian regime, and some other statements which were inaccurate, clearly exaggerated or which eventually proved to be false. And sixth, it seems striking to me that given all this, and within this scenario, secessionist parties got 47.8% of votes in the Catalan elections of 2015 (47.5% in the Catalan elections of 2017), and more than 2 million Catalans voted for secession in the October 1st 2017 referendum declared illegal by national authorities in which turnout was around 43%. At any event, this high percentage should not be sufficient for independence because secessionists are still a minority.

On the other hand, it is extremely striking that Mr. Rajoy took no political action at all. It is also striking that for tackling the Catalan secessionist conflict he relied exclusively on judges. To me, the first circumstance shows a blatant lack of leadership, which is supposed to be an essential taken for granted feature of politicians who rule a country. The second one is a risky policy because judges and courts are—in theory— independent and free from political pressures and therefore might render decisions which are not envisaged by governments or hamper their policies. And, besides, it puts the judiciary in the line of fire of indeed a legal case, but also of a political issue, and this might be detrimental to its institutional position. Later I will comment on some mistakes that Mr. Rajoy and his government committed.

In sum, these paradoxical and remarkable circumstances have led to an odd deadlock in which unilateral secession is not doable, or viable, and very likely it will not be so in the medium term. I do not think is necessary to insist on the fact that unilateral secession is completely out of reality. The unilateral declaration of independence of October 27th 2017 would not create a sovereign state with the ordinary attributes and features. A unilaterally and unlawfully seceded Catalonia would not be recognized by the most important occidental states and would not have international credit, at least among European states—as was said before, it would not automatically remain in the EU. It would not be able to develop real, working "statehood structures", as secessionists say. As I said before, the aspect that can be fairly considered most surprising is that this path-to-nowhere was consciously designed by a representative, democratically elected government and supported in the ballots by half of the Catalan voters.

And regarding a hypothetical agreed secession, it would not be possible at the moment of this writing (November 2018), for several, obvious reasons. First, and most importantly, because secession has not a majoritarian support—even less a "clear" majority, pursuant to the criterion of the Canadian Clarity Act. Second, because a hypothetical agreement at least on a process which would lead to secession would be considered contrary to the constitution, and therefore a constitutional amendment would be needed before the agreement. Third, because even if the agreement was constitutionally possible, the current political climate does not allow to foresee an appeasement which would allow the kind of political consensus needed to actually implement constitutional steps to secession. Fourth, because secession processes normally require time (the Québec bid started in the seventies, and is still going on), contrary to the extremely quick deadlines of the secessionists' road map.

2   Playing with Law and Politics

In the Catalan secessionist process law has been politically used by both sides. Indeed, it has been used by the national government led by Mr. Rajoy from 2012 to mid-2018, by alleging that the Spanish legal order—which clearly does not admit secession—is the only possible, monolithical response to the Catalan nationalist bloc, and therefore by assuming, and sometimes by openly stating, that this "law and order", rigid approach was the only way to deal with the conflict. This led in 2015 to a highly controversial, extremely quick amendment of the law pertaining to the Constitutional Court aimed at giving it powers to enforce its decisions such as fines, removal or substitution of officials which would fail to comply with the decisions, and prosecuting them for contempt. The amendment was clearly aimed at warning the Catalan leaders. Thus, former Catalan Presidents Mr. Mas was prosecuted for organizing the 2014 "consultation" and Mr. Puigdemont (and part of his government) were prosecuted for organizing the 2017 referendum. On the other hand, law has also been used by the Catalan government and by the secessionist bloc by endorsing a politically oriented interpretation of the international, European and national legal framework—a flawed interpretation, in my opinion and also according to most legal experts—and by unilaterally having triggered a secessionist process which was clearly and knowingly bound to a legal failure, and, at any event, that was bound to result in a confrontational, divisive outcome.

In that sense, Galán (2014: 905) argues that law has been disdained, and Fossas (2014) writes that both sides have trivialized the Constitution, and have politically appropriated or hijacked it: "*The Catalan Government has acted as if any witticism can fit in the Constitution, alleging that constitutional interpretation is not a juridical matter but a political one; and the national government has claimed that nothing can be done but to accept its own rigid interpretation of the Constitution, considered as immovable*". Thus, from 2012 to mid-2018 national authorities have used, and are still using, law to solve a political problem, which is not a wise thing to do, and Catalan secessionist have disregarded law by showing that they do not feel bound by the existing constitutional and legal framework—which they consider undemocratic, and by passing bills such as the "disconnection bills" from September 2017 which, as Ferreres et al. argue (2017), are clearly an insanity and a nonsense.

But even without this regrettable circumstance, it seems obvious to me that politics play a more important role than law in the understanding and in the possible solutions to the Catalan secessionist problem. In effect, referring to the Catalan question, Weiler (2012: 910) has written that "*the issue is not one of rights, of law*". More specifically, Sáiz Arnáiz (2006–2007: 50) stresses the inability of the judiciary, openly assumed in Canada, to solve the secessionist conflicts, and specifies that this means that courts cannot and should not decide on the clarity of a question in a referendum, or on an electoral majority or threshold. See also Vidmar's opinion (2017) about international law:

> Catalonia does not have a right to independence, and at the same time it is not doing anything illegal internationally when claiming or declaring independence. For better or worse, this is everything that the international law of statehood has to say on the matter. The rest is a political game.

This is not news, of course, but I find it important to reiterate that the problem is not (only) a legal or constitutional one, and that a hypothetical solution will not come from a legal reform or from a constitutional amendment. The problem, and its eventual solution, is mainly political, and I will now put some examples that reveal it. For instance, let's recall what the secessionist bloc consider five illegitimate mutilations of Catalonia's aspirations and self-government:

a. the amending in the national parliament of the revised "*Estatuto*" introduced by the Catalan parliament in 2005;

b. the 2010 judgment of the Constitutional Court that nullified part of the "*Estatuto*";
c. the barring of the "consultation" in 2014;
d. the barring of the referendum in 2017; and finally
e. the direct rule and emergency intervention that followed the unilateral declaration of independence, which dissolved the Catalan parliament, removed all the Catalan government and high ranking officials, and provoked the prosecution and incarceration of Catalan leaders and the exile of some of them.

All of these were normal consequences of the constitutional framework, although subject to political and ideological scrutiny and criticism, and were fairly predictable, for the Constitution and the laws were quite clear on these points. Perhaps the Constitutional Court might have avoided nullifying the mention that Catalonia was a "nation" (for example by considering it a "political" or symbolic statement lacking juridical content and not incompatible with article 2 of the constitution). But the fact that the Court did so, perhaps wrongly, does not mean, as López Bofill states (2018: 10) that it did deliberately put itself above the will of the Catalan people. And the emergency intervention of the Fall of 2017 might have avoided if the national government would have been willing to contemporize, or if Catalan leaders would not have deliberately pursued the "train crash" policy. So the arguments of the secessionist bloc are not in reality based on a disagreement with how law regulates the "*Estatuto*" and the alleged "right to decide". They disagree politically with the relationship between Catalonia and Spain and they do not seem to feel bound anymore by the constitutional founding pact of 1978 and by the consecutive legal rules.

This, as well as other circumstances, shows that law is not the problem, nor the solution. As the Constitutional Court clearly said in its 42/2014 judgment about the resolution of the Catalan parliament, mentioned in Chapter 2, Sect. 4, in some occasions law is not able to settle or to solve a particular political problem:

> The Constitution does not expressly cover, nor can it cover, all the issues that may arise in the constitutional order, particularly those derived from the wish of part of the State to alter its legal status. Issues of this kind cannot be resolved by the Court, whose task is to ensure that the Constitution is strictly complied with.

Neither side, particularly Mr. Rajoy during his two terms, seem to have read or to have understood what I consider the essential idea of the Canadian Supreme Court Reference of 1998, this main idea being that law by itself cannot solve social problems, even less when they have to do with identitarian perceptions and with nationalisms. This is why the main decisions in the secession procedure established in the Clarity Act, such as the decision to hold a referendum, the majority to consider that the territory is entitled to trigger the constitutional reform needed to achieve secession, etc. are not predetermined by law and, accordingly, are left to the political field. So the solution, if any, would need to be fruit of a political deal—although it is obvious that at the end of the day some kind of legal rules would have to be laid down to establish the new framework of the relationship between Spain and Catalonia, if there is to be one.

3   Relevant Mistakes Committed by Both Sides

I will now give my personal opinion on how both sides have dealt with the secessionist issue. I do not intend to be perfectly objective, non-judgmental or neutral, nor to defend the only correct constitutional or political interpretation of the conflict. But I do believe that when one, through arguments and reasons, makes explicit his subjectivity he might bring himself a little closer to objectivity.

As I explained before, the national government led by Mr. Rajoy stayed aloof and took no political action at all, and only gave a "law and order" response to secessionism. Nicolaïdis (2017) calls this attitude "simple, irreflexive legalism", and it could more precisely be called judicialism, because Mr. Rajoy decided to rely almost exclusively on prosecutions and on appeals to courts. Interestingly enough, judicialism has not disappeared with Mr. Rajoy, for in October 2018 Mr. Sánchez's government appealed to the Constitutional Court a resolution of the Catalan parliament which reproved the Monarchy. In my opinion the resolution was clearly political, in the sense that it had no legal content or effect at all, and the appeal was considered improper by the *Consejo de Estado*, the main board for legal advice. In spite of that, the national government filed the appeal. Galán writes (2014: 906) that Mr. Rajoy's policy "understood the constitution, and in general the legal framework as a rigid hammer" to be used against secessionists. Mr. Rajoy did precisely the opposite of what the Canadian Supreme Court stated in the 1998 Reference: "*The Constitution is not a straitjacket*" (paragraph 150).

Having said that, assessing how Mr. Rajoy handled the issue needs to be done carefully and distinguishing between different fields. Regarding the negotiations secessionists wanted to initiate, we should admit that Mr. Rajoy's position was not easy, for there was little margin (constitutionally or politically) for bargaining. When one of the parties has ceased to believe in the constitution as a whole (and not just in the territorial aspect), or—as happens with Mr. Torra's ideas which I quoted in Sect. 6 of Chapter 1—is openly insulting "the Spaniards", negotiation is extremely difficult indeed. So it was not realistic to expect or to require from the national government an open negotiation on secession, and I do not believe such kind of negotiation would take place in other EU countries with relevant secessionist pressure such as Belgium, or perhaps Italy. But, as I will comment later, Mr. Rajoy could have given some political credit to leaders which spoke in the name of almost 50% of Catalan voters. Or he could have at least initiated some kind of approximation or even of dialogue (not a negotiation or a bargain on the independence of Catalonia, which, as I just said, seems to me political science-fiction).

Second, to me the police action on the October 1st 2017 referendum was a mistake. Even if the decision was taken following the legal procedures, and pursuant to courts' decisions, sending the police to beat people which were queuing for voting was a very bad decision, both because of the mere fact of the beatings and—more importantly—because it was completely useless, for it did not prevent the referendum to take place. If you send the police to thwart the referendum you should make sure that poll stations would not open, or that people could not actually vote, etc., otherwise a partial police action would be useless, and would inevitably turn against the national government. And in my opinion this is exactly what happened. Actually, some individuals filed a criminal suit against the police officers, and in November 2018 the court has preliminary found that there were some specific excesses and that the beatings could be considered disproportioned—particularly given that the referendum was illegal and would have had no legal effects or at least the effects wanted by the organizers.[2]

Moreover, the photographs and footages of policemen beating voters on the referendum rapidly spread out the whole world, and whoever

[2]See https://www.lavanguardia.com/politica/20181108/452800673442/la-audiencia-censura-las-cargas-porque-el-1-o-no-tenia-efectos-juridicos.html.

viewed them might had thought that they had been taken in Venezuela, Nicaragua or other similar country. I am obviously not comparing Spain to these countries, but as a look to the international media reveal, this police action was worldwide perceived as an unjustified repressive excess similar to what usually happens in such countries. The national government was in part responsible of this because it did almost nothing to counteract this perception or to properly explain its decision of sending the police. Deliberately or just by clumsiness, Mr. Rajoy's government just let the images speak, and they clearly spoke against it. This provoked that the national government lost the narrative battle. The beatings might also have boosted the anti-democratic claim of secessionists, and some thought that it would fuel the anti-Spain perception in Catalonia (yet according to official statistics by the polling agency of the Catalan government, support for independence in Catalonia dropped from 42% in autumn 2017 to 38.8% in the spring of 2018).[3] In any case, the national government's inaction was quite surprising, and not just regarding the lack of reaction after the referendum, but also, for example, in relation to the main political or legal arguments of the secessionists.

Above all, and in a third level of analysis, Mr. Rajoy did not seem to acknowledge that there was a deep political problem in Catalonia—a problem that concerned him directly, among other things because his party was the fifth one in vote number in the Catalan elections of 2015, taking only 8.5% of the votes (in the 2017 Catalan elections it dropped to the seventh place, with 4.2%). An example of this aloof, "business as usual" attitude is that then-Vice President Mrs. Sáenz de Santamaría, after six hours of actual voting on the October 1st 2017 referendum, and after the police intervention, declared in an official press conference that "the referendum could not take place and has not taken place".[4] In my opinion, unless this statement is based in some kind of childish linguistic trick ("*only what I, Vice-President, consider a referendum and has been legally called by my government, is a referendum, otherwise it does not exist*"), it shows a serious confusion, because there was actually a referendum in which more than 2.200.000 persons voted. Indeed, it was a defective referendum with practically no independent oversight, and in which the police seized some ballot boxes and detained some activists,

---

[3] See http://upceo.ceo.gencat.cat/wsceop/6508/Abstract%20in%20English%20-874.pdf.
[4] See https://elpais.com/politica/2017/09/30/actualidad/1506768266_958938.html.

but a referendum after all, which police tried to prevent but could not. From this point of view, regardless of the turnout or of the actual outcome, October 1st 2017 cab fairly be considered a political defeat for Mr. Rajoy's government: secessionists wanted a referendum, and they had one (and they were able to disguise or to whisk away that it was illegal and defective and to showcase the beatings and the ballot box seizures as the unjustifiable repressive action of a non-democratic government). Actually, the wording of the European Commission's statement issued the day after the referendum was not without reason interpreted by the Catalan government as a criticism of the police action (*"Violence can never be an instrument in politics. We trust the leadership of Prime Minister Mariano Rajoy to manage this difficult process in full respect of the Spanish Constitution and of the fundamental rights of citizens enshrined therein"*).[5]

The Popular Party only reacted to the Catalan problem with law (and prosecutions), whereas it was clear to any fair spectator or analyst or citizen that politics and at least some dialogue were needed. Or, in any case, it seemed to see no need of any kind of constitutional pedagogy targeted not only to secessionists but also to non-secessionist Catalans and to ordinary Spaniards. Mr. Rajoy and the Popular Party did none of this and relied on legalism and on what can fairly be called judicialism—that is, resting on courts and on prosecutions. Trying to defeat an idea or an ideology (secessionism) only with a "law and order" policy is useless. Depicting Catalan secessionist politicians or voters, as most Spanish media did and as it reflected from some public official's statements, as illegitimate bearers of a heinous attempt of destroying Spain (and Europe) unworthy of political attention is probably as fictional as the secessionist virtual reality I will refer to in a moment. It is also politically unwise because it breaks the ties that sometime in the future will surely need to be rebuilt.

In any case, as Fossas (2014) has written, the promise of independence in 18 months starting from the 2015 Catalan elections was completely out of reality and absurd. This promise was both a mistake and a fiction. It was a mistake because promising as an achievable, feasible goal that independence would be obtained in the very short term, and

---

[5]See "Statement on the events in Catalonia", available at http://europa.eu/rapid/press-release_STATEMENT-17-3626_en.htm.

unilaterally, can fairly be deemed a political error—if we consider that promising or assuring what is blatantly impossible is, in politics, a mistake or a fraud. It was also an obvious fiction. Actually, it is not the only fiction Catalan secessionists have put up from 2012. They successfully sold to their electorate a virtual reality according to which, for example:

a. EU member states (at least some of them) would recognize Catalonia as an independent republic—which would remain in the EU;
b. Somewhat similarly, the Canadian model regarding Québec and the UK model regarding Scotland would be legitimate precedents, in any case applicable to Spain;
c. Spain is an undemocratic, totalitarian regime, still heir of Franco, which is breaching the democratic, collective rights of the Catalan people;
d. Catalonia has one voice—and only one—which is pro secession;
e. After direct rule, and after the prosecution of Catalan leaders, Catalonia is undergoing a "humanitarian crisis"; and
f. Direct rule impeded independence, which would have been achieved if the national government wouldn't have triggered the emergency measures.

All this is a fictional narration. Of course, as I will, argue in the next paragraph the notion of democracy and of democratic behavior is debatable, and depicting Spain as an undemocratic, totalitarian regime is not accurate at all. It is also unfair, because "Spain" (that is, the political system based in the 1978 constitution) has brought Catalonia to its maximum level of self-government, freedom and prosperity ever. Besides, some specific parts of the narration might be tricky. For instance, appealing to the Canadian and British solutions and alleging that they are applicable to Spain can only be done if one deliberately ignores the obvious constitutional and political differences, as was explained in Chapter 2. And, as Romero Caro has pointed out (2017), this is based on a misinterpretation of the Clarity Act because secessionists adduce that the Canadian model entitles them to the "right to decide" construed as the right to have a referendum on independence, and, if secession prevails on the ballots, then independence is automatic. Both things are false. And nevertheless the national government did nothing to combat or to challenge this distorted "Canadian narrative". Futhermore, it is also false that it was direct rule which prevented independence, and which prevented the Catalan republic to be born. It was rather the self-evident unviability of gaining actual sovereignty. I mean that even without the emergency intervention of the national government, a unilaterally seceded Catalonia would not have had international and EU recognition, would not have had the possibility of creating a legal citizenship and other features of statehood, and probably would not have had access to international financial markets and would could place its debt bonds, etc.

Choosing Mr. Torra as President of Catalonia in May 2018 can fairly be deemed a mistake, or at least a shockingly unwise decision. I am referring to his supremacist insults and utterances against "Spain" and "Spaniards" I mentioned in Sect. 6 of Chapter 1 (he used the terms hyenas, vipers, beasts, fascist-like, etc.). What would most Catalans say if national parties or national parliament chose as Prime Minister someone that wittingly and publicly says such things against "Catalonia" and against "Catalans". Would they not consider it unacceptable? Well, the Catalan parliament appointed (and Catalans seemed to accept) as President a person with absolutely unacceptable ideas, and this reveals the profound degradation of the political situation in Catalonia.

Galán (2014: 900) has convincingly argued that both sides have over-simplified the issues—this has been particularly present in the secessionist side. For example, when announcing the October 2017 referendum, Catalan secessionist leaders insisted on the fact that the EU would back a seceded Catalonia, which would remain in the EU—both things were not true. In reality, the three different levels of the EU issue were swiped from the debate, these three levels being:

a. whether unilateral secession was compatible with EU law—it is not;
b. whether a territory that would have seceded would automatically remain as a member state—it would not and
c. whether the seceded territory would have some kind of fast-track, privileged status in the accession procedure (articles 48 or 49 TEU)—surely this would depend on the fact that secession would be agreed or not.

Around the secessionist process there has been a striking lack of clarity, somewhat similarly to what happened in the *Brexit* referendum in 2016. In both cases—in my opinion, much more in Spain than in the UK—the reality regarding the UE or the secession scenarios was completely out of the debate and the campaign. Real, profound debate was hijacked by both sides. Secessionists hijacked the debate on the EU, on the majority needed to proclaim and obtain independence, and of course on specific economic and social issues and on how an independent Catalonia would deal with them. Mr. Rajoy's government, and most unionists, hijacked any kind of political debate on dialogue and consensus, and denied political recognition to what they seemed to consider an evil enemy.

Besides, secessionists have confounded two different things: the social or electoral majority needed to claim for a referendum (and eventually to obtain it), on the one hand, and the social or electoral majority needed for secession, on the other. They seem to believe that the fact of around 50% of voters supporting secessionist parties, and that according to polls an even higher percentage want an agreed referendum, mean that they were and still are entitled to secession. To me, this is wrong. The first majority (the one need to seek and eventually obtain a referendum) does not need to be superior to 50%, and it would indeed constitute, as López Bofill says (2018: 5), a strong popular pressure sufficient to at least ground a legitimate political demand. Inversely, the second majority, the one needed in a referendum on secession, needs to be a "clear majority", as the Canadian Clarity Act established. And, above all, and even in case a clear majority pro secession is reached in an eventual referendum, none of the two foreign models constantly invoked (Canada and the UK) entitles the territory to automatic, unconditional secession but only gives right to initiate negotiations with the national authorities. Catalan secessionists deliberately misinterpreted the foreign precedents and mixed up the majority for a referendum and the majority for secession—probably because they knew there would be no agreed referendum and therefore the second majority would never be seriously tested.

It is legitimate to wonder why Catalan secessionist politicians have led Catalonia to an independence process which was, and still is, clearly impossible to achieve. In this aspect emerge the differences between the Scotland and Québec processes and the Catalan process. In the latter it was out of doubt that there would be no agreement with national authorities and that there would be a deadlock. By deadlock I am referring to a situation in which it appears impossible that any of the parties can make their ideas prevail, or can take steps towards achieving their goal. It is impossible—practically, politically, internationally—that Catalonia unilaterally becomes an independent state and be so recognized. And it seems impossible that only with a "law and order" policy the national government can revert the situation and bring back half of the Catalan voters to the constitution.

As I said, it is also legitimate to wonder whether Mr. Mas (President of Catalonia from 2010 to 2015), Mr. Puigdemont (President from January 2016 to October 2017), and lately Mr. Torra (President from May 2018) were and still are aware of this dead end, and, if so, if they were and still are playing some kind of foolish challenge or bluff, aimed not at obtaining independence—for it was evident that it would not be actually be achieved—but at forcing the national authorities to concessions such as, for instance, more political power or a new fiscal regime. In June 2018 Mrs. Ponsatí, a former member of the Catalan government who flew to Scotland to avoid being sent to prison, answered the question and denuded the whole secessionist agenda: "*We were bluffing.*"[6]

In sum, my belief is that both unilateralism and legalism or judicialism are grave mistakes which will have serious consequences. Catalan leaders pushed an agenda based on unilateral secession, which was and still is not only contrary to the constitution but, above all, completely undoable and out of reality. The national government, in order to tackle the secessionist issue, took no political action at all and relied only on legalistic arguments. And in fact it seemed to assume no responsibility and relied on courts. So in my opinion both sides committed mistakes—and actually, in some cases, the same mistakes. Part of the media, of scholars and of intellectuals were with good reason blaming on Mr. Rajoy that he was unduly dogmatic, too stringent and unwilling to give in or to acknowledge any kind of political credit to secessionists, etc., but these features can be attributed to secessionists, which followed a somewhat radical, "*we shall not be moved*" approach (Mr. Junqueras, Catalan Vice-President until the national government imposed direct rule, authored an article (2017) titled "*Catalonia will not retreat*"). Both sides seem to have risen up to a categorical imperative their political positions or aspirations.

Was all this a deliberate option? Walker believes so. Regarding the UK and Scotland, and this was much more evident in Spain and Catalonia, he writes (2015: 5) that there was "a strategically measured—some might say cynical—political opportunism (on all sides) that takes the line of most convenience". In the Catalan case this means that both sides seem to have spoken only to one fraction of the population (Spanish

---

[6] See https://elpais.com/ccaa/2018/06/09/catalunya/1528573971_502571.html.

or Catalan), and that they have not even tried to establish a common ground of understanding and of respect for the opponent.

I will finish this section by clarifying that the problem is not in the constitution, nor in the allegedly lack of democratic feature of the Spanish regime. The constitution, overwhelmingly ratified by Catalans in 1978, establishes the sovereignty of the whole nation and its indivisibility—just like other European constitutions such as the French, the Italian and the German do. And it creates a modern, democratic, decentralized, human rights abiding political system which cannot be seriously deemed as totalitarian or undemocratic. Rather, the problem might rather be the attitude adopted by the national government from 2012 to mid-2018 and by Catalan secessionists. Indeed, banning a referendum and sending policemen to beat voters (which, as said earlier, I consider a mistake), and prosecuting and incarcerating without trial the main secessionist politicians, even if technically has been done pursuant to the Criminal Code, might not fit in what some might consider a democratic behavior. Actually, it has been easily sold as "undemocratic" by Catalan secessionists, and might not have happened in some other European states, less rigid in the use of prison without bail. But all this does not make Spain, and its constitution, a totalitarian, undemocratic state.

But, as I have been arguing, Mr. Rajoy not wanting to grant political credit to secessionists (and his shocking clumsiness in explaining his governments' position, and uselessly beating voters and demonstrators) might have boosted the secessionists "antidemocratic argument", according to which by denying and banning a referendum on independence, an undemocratic "Spain" was trampling a "democratic" Catalonia. I will discuss now the democratic augment.

4   Secession and Democracy

The most interesting aspect of the conflict is that both sides have appealed to democracy. Unionists as well as secessionists claim that "democracy" is on their side. It is legitimate to wonder whether both sides are using competing visions of democracy. Of course, there exist different notions or criteria of "democracy", and of political representation, and most occidental democracies have not-so-democratic features. Some classic examples, of course each one with a different level of "undemocracy", are the electoral college in the US presidential elections (which provoke, for instance, that incumbent President Trump lost the 2016 elections measured by popular votes instead of by electoral votes); the "*winner takes all*" majoritarian electoral system in the UK, and in other countries, which leaves minorities infra-represented; or the excesses of some Westminster models, which allow Parliaments to choose as Prime Minister a non-elected person—as has happened in Italy in the last years with Prime Ministers Monti, Letta, Renzi, Gentiloni and Conte, and has also happened in Spain in 2018 with Prime Minister Sánchez (although the case is slightly different, because he had previously been a member of parliament).

At any event, I do not think the "democratic" argument is conclusive. Indeed, secessionist have a point when they claim that not allowing a referendum is undemocratic. As Vilajosana suggests (2014), this political discourse should not be underestimated—and this is what the national government did from 2012 to mid-2018. On the other hand, unionists have a point when they claim that there has been no democracy breach because Catalan people freely spoke in 1978 (when they almost unanimously voted for the constitution which laid sovereignty in the Spanish people and not in the Catalan people), in 1979 (when they ratified in referendum their first "*Estatuto*") and in 2006 (when they ratified in referendum the second "*Estatuto*"). And in the three occasions Catalans freely and democratically accepted the constitutional system or the "*Estatuto*" that is at the base of their self-government. Both claims of "democracy", particularly the secessionists', have a pre-juridical basis, as happens with everything related to nationalism, and therefore legal and constitutional reasoning may not be as useful in terms of democracy as both sides argue.

Are those two competing visions of democracy? I do not think so, at least not in a philosophical, profound meaning, and at least as it derives from the standpoint taken by secessionists and by unionists. I tend to believe that both sides have calculatedly used the notion of democracy which best suited their interests. One of the mistakes both sides committed was not to start a serious, moral debate on the common *demos*, on the political consensus and on the constitution, and therefore their allegations regarding democracy are, as Walker argues, in general closer to opportunism and to empty clichés than to serious, candid political reasoning.

For instance, one might have thought that this was a good occasion to initiate a serious dialogue on the idea of the nation and on its constitutional reflection. Or a debate on whether the constitutional territorial consent, interpreted as irreversible, is compatible or not with some notions of democracy. It is perfectly legitimate to believe that a perpetual, irredeemable constitutional or collective bond is not democratic, just like Jefferson wrote in 1789, in a famous letter to Madison, that each generation should have the right to decide their own present, because "no society can make a perpetual constitution, or even a perpetual law" and because "the earth belongs to the living, and not to the dead". But, as far as I know, none of this has been mentioned in Spain since the Catalan conflict started. Little has been said, in the press or in Parliament, or even in academic milieus, that comes near to the moral, social, historical and constitutional debate Canadians had between 1995 (the second referendum) and 2000 (the Clarity Act).[7] From his point of view, the situation in Spain is somewhat disheartening.

Nevertheless, probably there exist some different perceptions of the constitution, as the traditional monist notion, with a single narrative, or rather as an open, pluralistic or even multi-national concept. Keating (2012: 13–14) thinks that this might be the real problem, Romano (2018: 53 ff.) argues about territorial co-sovereignty, and Caamaño (2014) contends that the traditional notion of sovereignty is not valid anymore to understand modern, pluralist o plurinational societies based on what he calls "*demoicracy*", nor to solve identitarian or territorial problems. If this is the underlying essential problem, and I believe it might be so, then the 2017 experts' report (Muñoz Machado 2017: 8) would be right when it speaks about a "dissociation between democracy and the constitution". In the Catalan conflict, as happens frequently when "the nation" (or exclusive nationalism) is involved, some kind of friction is growing between constitutional rule of law and democracy, and it is getting closer to a dangerous zero-sum game (López Bofill 2018: 3).

Of course Aláez (2015: 143) is right when he argues that the territorial debate should not necessarily lead to a clash between respecting the constitution and respecting the democratic principle except, he adds, in case of a non-juridical vision of democracy and of its subjects. Well, this pre-juridical, identitarian notion of democracy is precisely the issue when nationalism appears. Identitarian nationalism might not acknowledge

---

[7]See, for example, the hearings previous to the Act in the Legislative Committee of the House of Commons part of which are available at http://www.revparl.ca/23/2/23n2_00e_Dion.pdf.

as "democratic" a constitutional framework in which it has no space to become a "nation", or a "state", and in which the *demos* is not accepted. By *demos* I mean the definition of the nation and of the boundaries and nature of the political community—and, from a legal point of view, maybe also the mere idea of constituent power.

Was that the Spanish government's attitude undemocratic, as secessionists, and scholars such as Ridao and González, and López Bofill suggest? In my opinion, it was not per se undemocratic, but, as the latter writes (2018: 3), it entails democratic deficits (in the sense that it could have shown much more flexibility and even some kind of approximation to secessionists). Let's not forget that negotiation, or at least dialogue, is an essential element of politics, and the Popular Party's government clearly neglected it. To me, it even neglected listening to secessionists, and it should have at least done it—even if what they wanted was blatantly contrary to the constitution. If modern democracies (particularly in multicultural countries, or in countries with territorial nationalisms, or even in countries with a multilevel governance system) need to be deliberative and at least relatively open, then the lack of dialogue and recognition showed by Mr. Rajoy's government can indeed be considered flawed from this democratic point of view. Moreover, as Caamaño suggests (2014: 223), by openly stating that only its view of "the nation" (backed by the 2010 judgement of the Constitutional Court regarding the "*Estatuto*") is acceptable, the national government has monopolized, or absolutized, the idea of the constitutional consensus—or at least its core. When facing the secessionist challenge, Mr. Rajoy and the Popular Party failed to effectively defend and to promote the integrative values of the constitution, and this was disappointing to many non-secessionists.

With the permission of Kelsen, the national government is the immediate guarantor of the constitution, and the constitution is not just "law and order", it is—it should be—a collective consensus which should be based on persuasion and be attained through ideas and recognition. Apparently, Mr. Rajoy and the Popular Party conceived the constitution, and the consensus it is based on, as a weapon or as straitjacket, and did not attempt to use it as an integrative tool aimed at promoting a "counterbalancing ethos of dialogue and respect" (Nicolaïdis 2017). I am fully aware of the difficulties of creating such a spirit in times of confrontation, and when secessionists to not feel bound by the constitution and seem to despise everything coming from Spain. But it was—and still is—worth trying, and to me there was no serious try at all.

As for the criticism according to which Mr. Rajoy's government, and in general the Popular Party, criminalized secession, or even dissent towards the constitution, I don't think so. But it is true that when prosecuting the Catalan leaders after the 2017 referendum, it interpreted the Criminal Code in a strict, repressive way, and many consider legally unfounded the accusation of rebellion (and probably also of sedition). It is also true that in the Popular Party's background there is a whiff of this kind of abuse of criminal law (for instance on the occasion of the passing of the political parties bill of 2002, when not condemning terrorism by members of parties was considered a secondary evidence for banning the party, or its insistence of considering a crime hard, critical political speech consisting in booing at the national anthem in football stadiums, or in burning pictures of the King, or the Spanish flag—or blowing one's nose with it).

Was the EU's attitude undemocratic because it did not support a referendum on secession in Catalonia? Was there a violation of the democratic and human rights principles enshrined in article 2 TUE? I think the answer to both questions is "no", for the reasons I briefly stated in Chapter 2, Sect. 5, and for the following arguments. The claim that the EU should initiate actions against Spain pursuant to article 7 TUE, as Ridao and González suggest (2014: 376) is not only flawed because of a non-existent breach of article 2 TUE, it is only clearly exaggerated if compared with the use the UE has done of this article regarding Poland and Hungary. Despite all the mistakes committed by Mr. Rajoy's government, I do not think that the government itself, the Parliament and the Constitutional Court violated EU law nor EU democratic values or principles for not allowing a referendum on independence in Catalonia. The Spanish constitution fully complies with democratic, human rights standards, it respects and tolerates political ideas and dissent, and allows democratic political participation. And it grants to Catalonia, and to the other "*Comunidades Autónomas*", a high level of self-government. Furthermore, the main characteristics of a nation (self-government, elected parliament, own official language, police, flag, anthem, taxes) have already been granted to Catalonia. If a concrete form of referendum does not fit into the constitution, then there exist democratic processes aimed at amending it in order to allow the referendum (indeed, as I will mention in next chapter, the amendment procedures are legally burdensome and some of them are politically out of any realistic scenario). Of course secessionists can validly claim that they were non-violently seeking democracy, and all they wanted was to be able to vote, but the fact that they were not allowed to do it, that some voters were beaten and that Catalan self-government was suspended is not, in my opinion, tantamount to a brutal reaction which contained serious violations of human rights that have no comparison within the occidental, liberal democracies, as López Bofill argues (2018: 16). Besides, should Ridao and González be right, then Germany and Italy would be non-democratic countries as well, and would also have violated EU law—even taking into account that, as I mentioned before, German and Italians realities are different from what is going on in Catalonia because political pressure in favour or secession is clearly smaller.

Regarding the EU aspect of the Catalan conflict, Closa (2016: 249) argues that the main stands of secessionists (automatic accession of seceded territories and member states breaching article 2 TUE if they do not allow referenda or secession) "rely on a shallow conception of democracy, whereby democracy becomes a simply majoritarian principle prevailing over any other consideration". This is an important idea and I am going to bring it to the Spanish secessionist debate. If, as secessionists claim, what is at stake is democracy, and accordingly Mr. Rajoy's government attitude was at least partially undemocratic, which can be assumed as a dialectical hypothesis, then Catalan secessionists' attitude was, and still is, undemocratic as well.

First, because deliberately ignoring or breaking a liberal, democratic constitution (which was almost unanimously accepted by Catalan voters in 1978) is not a democratic attitude. In democratic, human rights abiding states, and in which no oppression or blatant injustice is present, appealing to democratic legitimacy against, above or without the law is not acceptable. As Ferreres et al. argue (2017), justifying and claiming as valid unilateral "disconnection" reveals a profound contempt for the essentials rules of a democratic legal order. So the Catalan secessionist's attitude is undemocratic because they "pushed the unilateral way to independence based on an idea of the democratic principle taken as an absolute criterion which allows them to contravene the constitution and the 'Estatuto', and to dissociate democracy and the constitution" (Muñoz Machado 2017: 8). Secessionists have acted as if democracy was possible, or legitimate, without the rule of law.

Second, because practically blaming all the problems on "Spain" and doing away from the electoral and social scenario every collective, political issue (such as education, unemployment, economy, welfare, etc.), and focusing the whole political debate on secession from Spain is to me undemocratic either because it creates an artificial Leviathan or because it despises the real problems people have and it leaves people without real, free political options. The national government has been accused, and with good reason, of not having played politics when dealing with the secessionist process, but this is also true for secessionists: since 2010 or 2012 they have almost played no politics or implemented no policies at all, because they had in mind only the secessionist bid. Taking "Spain" as the origin of all the grievances of "Catalonia" has led, among other things, to a nonsense victimization and to building a friend/foe confrontation between "Spain" and "Catalonia", as if the latter was monolithically pro secession—which is absolutely fictitious and undemocratic. It has led as well at shushing or at pointing accusing fingers at Catalans which do not support secession. As happens frequently with identitarian nationalism, the "nation" drive has been used at least by the most radical as a collective, undemocratic alibi to supress or at least to silence dissent, or in some cases to stigmatise non-secessionists as bad, anti-patriotic Catalans.

And third, and above all, Catalan secessionists have undemocratically behaved because, as Sarmiento (2018) rightly argues, "secessionists attempted to impose a new legal order to the entire Catalan population knowing as they did that they lacked a majority".

Indeed, secessionists would reply that precisely the stubborn, stringent prohibition of any kind of consultation or referendum impeded them from legally and legitimately show that they were backed by a sufficient majority of the population. Accordingly, they would argue that they had no other option, and that theirs was a legitimate reaction to a previous, much more serious breach of democracy committed by an intransigent national government. Even giving some minimal credit to this argument, the undisputable fact is that declaring independence with only 48% of popular votes (as Tables 1 and 2 shown in Chapter 1, around 2.000.000 persons voted for secessionist parties in the Catalan elections 2015 and 2017 and voted "Yes" in the October 1st 2017 referendum) does not seem to me consistent with any notion of democracy.

May I insist that both sides have had, one way or another, some kind of undemocratic behaviour. Nevertheless, in my opinion the main breaches of democracy (and of course of the rule of law) have been committed by the secessionists—but this by no means gives credit to Mr. Rajoy's policies of denying recognition to them.

5   IS THERE A WAY OUT?

5.1   The Need for Dialogue and Mutual Recognition

This leads me to the main point, this main point being trying to find proposals, or a common ground, for a constructive way out of the crisis. The path to solution, or at least to unlock the deadlock, needs to be based on recognizing the political legitimacy of the other side, and probably on dialogue. This has been repeatedly pointed out by authors such as Presno (2015) and Nicolaïdis (2017), and lately by the experts and scholars' proposal for a constitutional reform proposal led by Muñoz Machado (speaking about the necessity of a "reencounter"). The idea was also included in the "Statement on the events in Catalonia" issued by the European Commission on October 2nd 2017: "We call on all relevant players to now move very swiftly from confrontation to dialogue."[8]

It might seem surprising that both things (dialogue and respecting disagreement) need to be reminded, for they should be present as a pre-requisite in any democratic political process or debate. This reveals the deep incomprehension, entrenchment and partisanship that has been going on at least since 2012, and probably since the 2006 "*Estatuto*", and not just between the national government and the Catalan government, but also between the main national parties.

It is obvious that the goal of this new approach would necessary be, using Nicolaïdis expression, mutual political recognition, and by that I mean an attitude based on tolerance, engagement, deference, trust and acknowledgment that the other side bears the representation of citizens. Its aim should be the reconstruction of a minimum social, political and constitutional consensus in Catalonia, which around half of Catalan leaders and voters consider broken. In a famous newspaper op-ed Former Prime Minister Felipe González (2015) stated that "*we badly need a compromise for reforms which would guarantee the 'differentiative facts' without breaking citizenship equality all over Spain nor the collective sovereignty to decide our common future*". In any case, it is self-evident that the path to mutual understanding between Spanish constitutionalists (or unionists) and Catalan secessionists would start at least by initiating a dialogue (which has not happened between 2012 and mid-2018, for national

---

[8] See http://europa.eu/rapid/press-release_STATEMENT-17-3626_en.htm.

government led by Mr. Rajoy and Catalan government led by Mr. Mas and lately by Mr. Puigdemont have not met nor have attempted to do it) and by ceasing partisan use of the constitution and of the media.

I would like to clarify that by "dialogue" I do not mean a negotiation or bargaining on secession, which would be contrary to the constitution and is out of the political scenario in Spain, and to which Catalan secessionist leaders are not per se entitled, as Walker admits (2015: 8) when writing that "Even though there continues to be no automatic entitlement absent a standing injustice, the articulation of a desire for independence on the part of a sub-state national group, ideally through the mechanism of referendum, should be sufficient to trigger a requirement on the part of the existing state to negotiate in good faith with the sub-state nation over their aspirations for independence". What I am referring to is the need that both sides take steps towards some kind of reconstruction of a common political ground. This is not news. It was explicitly written in the Canadian 1998 Supreme Court Reference regarding constitutional amendment: "*Our democratic institutions necessarily accommodate a continuous process of discussion and evolution, which is reflected in the constitutional right of each participant in the federation to initiate constitutional change. This right implies a reciprocal duty on the other participants to engage in discussions to address any legitimate initiative to change the constitutional order*" (paragraph 150).

The political reconstruction of a minimum social and constitutional consensus should be the aim of both sides. The first step for mutual recognition and for the compromise sought by former Prime Minister González would consist in both sides backing out at least partially. Unionists and secessionists would have to admit errors, to acknowledge some political credit to the opponent, and to abandon the radical friend/ foe approach, and this would be relatively unusual in Spanish politics, in which appears frequently a confrontational idea of democracy. This is why compromise, or at least some kind of appeasement, is very unlikely for the time being because in the last years both sides have maintained radical positions. Moreover, in many of their statements and positions it is easy to perceive rancor (institutional, partisan, territorial, identitarian rancor) or, as Nicolaïdis writes (2017), "a downward spiral towards an abyss of mutual acrimony". What seems to present is many parties, media and civil society is some kind of comfort in situations of confrontation and victimization, as if the democratic malaise in contemporary Spain had appeared and had focused in the Catalan conflict.

Hence, it is difficult to be optimistic regarding recognition and compromise. On the one hand, Catalan secessionist leaders have promoted a profound social movement which is very difficult to stop (and even if the leaders back out, it could be probably socially perceived as cowardice and as a shameful surrender). On the other hand, the national government has followed from 2012 to mid-2018 a "law and order" agenda which, they seem to think, is the only possibility and will give them electoral credit at least at national level. This agenda has spread the idea, which I consider wrong, that no agreement or dialogue would be constitutionally valid or politically possible, and has boosted and externalized a nationalistic feeling in Spain, which was perhaps present, or dormant, and had not shown in the last two or three decades. As I said, many people in Spain (politicians, and hooligan-like supporters in the media and in citizenry) would probably see this recoil or this compromise as a defeat.

Once the psychological and political mechanisms of confrontational nationalism, victimization and denial of recognition have been triggered, there are enormous difficulties to rebuild a collective, general consensus, both at Catalan and at national level. This is true for any country experiencing nationalism, radical or not, but I think it is particularly serious when the political climate is so severely deteriorated as it is in Spain. Things would probably be different without some unsatisfactory features of the Spanish democratic system and its troubling difficulties to deal with corruption, with territorial diversity, with excessive powers of political parties, with independent media, and with respecting the independence of the judiciary. Mutual recognition, that is, a reciprocal duty of respecting the rival's approach and accepting some legitimacy of the other side, is difficult when, as appears to be the case in Spain, political élites are bitterly entrenched and partisan, and show a worrying absence of capability, or will, to generate collective consensus and to reach agreements and compromises in essential matters. This seems to me the main—and saddest—difference between the Catalan secessionist process and the Québec and Scotland precedents. The latter were difficult, of course, but did not create such a bitter, divisive social breakup.

Of course, during the Transition (1975–1978) circumstances were also very difficult (in some aspects more difficult than now, because of the resilience of franquism and because of terrorism, military coups, economic stress, no institutional settlement, no democratic tradition, etc.), and nevertheless an enormous social consensus was reached which "permitted to get rid of 'the two Spains' and of partisan constitutions"

(Muñoz Machado 2017: 12). Despite some perhaps doubtful aspects, the Spanish Transition was considered an example all over the world, lasted many years, and produced a constitution equatable to the modern European constitutions and, above all, contributed decisively to the spectacular transformation of Spain in an advanced democratic society. Thus, Spaniards were capable of overcoming confrontation and of generating a wide, lasting social consensus. Will we be willing to do it again?

5.2   The Viability of Constitutional Reform(s) and the Possible Acknowledgement of the Plurinationality of Spain

Recapitulating what I pointed out in Chapter 2, Sect. 4, from a legal or constitutional point of view, the situation seems to be quite clear. Because article 2 of the constitution stipulates that the nation or the state is unitarian and indivisible, and that sovereignty lies in the whole Spanish people, it prohibits the "right to decide" aimed at holding a regional referendum on independence—and of course it prohibits also unilateral secession. Therefore, no territory or region can validly hold a referendum on independence nor subsequently declare itself independent from Spain. Same goes for federal countries such as the US, Mexico, Germany, Australia, and for non-federal countries as well such as Italy. The right to self-determination, as framed in the UN treaties, does not apply to Catalonia, for it was aimed, in the 1950s and the 1960s, at fostering decolonization. Regarding a hypothetical referendum, according to the mainstream political and scholar opinion, the constitution forbids the national government to reach an agreement with the Catalan government in order to hold a referendum about independence or about the political status of Catalonia in Spain, as then-Prime Minister Cameron did regarding Scotland in 2013. The existing constitutional framework does not allow secession, nor a referendum (even an agreed referendum). Hence, as the Spanish Constitutional Court stated in its 42/2014 judgement, the only possible way to admit a referendum on secession—and eventually secession—would be a constitutional amendment.

So there appears to be only two possibilities. One is doing nothing (politically), as was Mr. Rajoy's policy from 2012 to mid-2018, and wait until eventually Catalan secessionists return to their previous positions, abandon unilateralism and insurrection and accept the constitutional status quo. The other one would be a constitutional reform. For obvious reasons I am not discussing the first one, which I just said I consider a mistake. This makes constitutional reform the only real option. As the 2017 experts report argues, "paralysis or the incapacity to tackle constitutional reforms jeopardizes the whole political system" (Muñoz Machado 2017: 10).

This second possibility could in turn consist in a complete constitutional reform which would allow secession, or, on the contrary, in a partial reform, or arrangement, that would not allow secession but would appease at least part of the secessionist voters.

Let's focus first in the "complete reform" scenario. From a strictly legal perspective the only way to channel a hypothetical secessionist process, including a referendum, would be a constitutional amendment. Surprisingly enough, the Spanish constitution seems to permit an amendment which would consist in creating a procedure aimed at achieving the secession of a part of the country. The Constitutional Court openly admitted it in its 42/2014 ruling (see Chapter 2, Sect. 4) by leaving open the door for accepting the "right to decide", whatever it means, and perhaps a path to secession, but only after a constitutional reform. This is correct from a strictly juridical, technical perspective. Unlike in the US or Germany or Australia, Spain's constitution has no "eternity clause", or "perpetual bond", and therefore any constitutional amendment or revision is possible, even if it divides Spain or it allows one of its parts to unilaterally decide its secession or, as in Canada, it establishes some kind of agreed procedure—if channeled through the specific amendment process. But in practical terms this reform is extremely difficult to achieve because it would need to be channeled through the "hard" amendment process. The constitution provides for two different amendment processes: a "soft" or "ordinary" one in article 167 and a "hard" or "extraordinary" one, applicable to the main constitutional structures and principles and regulated in article 168. An amendment which would divide Spain or allow a territory to secede would need to be channeled through article 168, which states:

> 1. If a total revision of the Constitution is proposed, or a partial revision thereof, affecting the Preliminary Title, Chapter Two, Section 1 of Title I, or Title II, the principle shall be approved by a two-hirds majority of the members of each House, and the Cortes shall immediately be dissolved. 2. The Houses elected must ratify the decision and proceed to examine the new Constitutional text, which must be approved by a two thirds majority of the members of both Houses. 3. Once the amendment has been passed

by the Cortes Generales [*the national Parliament*], it shall be submitted to ratification by referendum.

So after a first political decision of amending the constitution (the "principle"), a new Parliament has to accept it and draft the new text, which needs to be ratified through a referendum at national level. It is quite clear, as Tornos Mas has written (2017: 77) that the "extraordinary" amendment is in fact a new constitution, or at least is tantamount to a constituent process.

This would be the orthodox way out of the conflict, and the amendment procedure and the resulting constitutional wording have been impeccably suggested by Aláez (2015). Yet the political and legal problems make this amendment undoable. In my opinion this possibility is completely out of the political reality, and not just because of the enormous, overwhelming hurdles of the amendment procedure of article 168 of the constitution, or for the inexistence of a political climate in which starting a collective dialogue aimed a constitutional reform, at least for the time being. The amendment is unfeasible mainly because even if this climate of dialogue existed, it would be science-fictional to envisage that it would be channeled to an amendment which would legalize secession of a territory. I mean that even if the amendment process would be triggered, it would be extremely unlikely that a national consensus would be reached (three times) about allowing Catalonia, or any other part of Spain, to initiate a secessionist process. This kind of amendment is clearly out of the political horizon in Spain, and probably also in most countries.

So if the "complete reform" scenario is not viable, maybe a "partial reform" could be tried. This second possibility would consist in a political arrangement in form of a constitutional reform which would not include a referendum, and a path to secession, but would acknowledge the singularity of Catalonia (that is, the so-called "differentiative fact"), would eventually allow the national parliament to introduce some asymmetrical status to some *Comunidades Autónomas* such as Catalonia, and would perhaps admit that Catalonia is a nation. Let's see how this proposal was built.

The arrangement idea was launched by the socialist party in 2013, with the so-called "Granada Declaration",[9] but it was only a draft or a

---

[9] See http://web.psoe.es/source-media/000000562000/000000562233.pdf.

political proposal which would define the party's territorial strategy. It was followed in a much more articulated, non-political fashion by prestigious scholars such as Muñoz Machado (2014, 2016) and Tornos Mas (2014, 2015, 2017), and, somewhat differently, as Caamaño (2014). All these works have in common a non-partisan approach, and are based on the belief that a partial constitutional reform is both desirable and inevitable, and therefore that something needs to be done in order to rebuild the constitutional and political consensus. Muñoz Machado's proposal of 2014 was widely disseminated and, in part, supported by some media and some politicians, and would consist first in a constitutional amendment (in the terms I will detail immediately), which would include a referendum at national level, and second in an adjustment of the legal and institutional relationship between Catalonia and Spain (likely with a new "Estatuto"), which would also require a referendum (at Catalan level).

The ideas of Muñoz Machado and Tornos Mas were assumed by a group of scholars (which included both of them) who in November 2017 produced a report titled "Ideas for a constitutional reform" (Muñoz Machado 2017). This initiative is a serious, articulated proposal for a constitutional amendment, and consists in:

- first, a general constitutional reform which would transform Spain into a federal state by a new distribution of powers and competences between the Federation and the "*Comunidades Autónomas*", by making the Senate become a real territorial chamber, as it is for example in Germany, and by establishing a new financing system (which as for now is practically deconstitutionalized);
- second, a more specific reform aimed at acknowledging some "*differentiative facts*" or asymmetries regarding the "*nationalities*" mentioned in article 2 of the constitution. This would allow Catalonia some singularities within the Spanish federation, to recover part of the contents of the 2006 "*Estatuto*" nullified by the Constitutional Court and to include in its future "*Estatuto*" specific identitarian aspects.

In the summer of 2017, during the harshest period of the Catalan crisis, Mr. Sánchez (just reelected general secretary of the socialist party) started to speak of the necessity of acknowledging that Spain is a "nation of nations" and therefore that Catalonia is a nation—but within an indissoluble Spain. Then the socialist congress passed a declaration, the so called "Barcelona declaration", which would define Spain a plurinational state, or as a "nation of nations". But this idea, even after being publicly fostered by Mr. Sánchez, has not been assumed as the party's official view in the proposal of constitutional reform adopted in early 2018.[10]

This partial reform might certainly have some effect, because of its symbolic content (and eventually because of the recognition of Catalonia as a nation, which has always been a very relevant issue). As I said, its aim seems to be persuading the less radical secessionists to abandon unilateralism, to back to their previous political stand and to accept this new constitutional federal model. Tornos Mas is very clear on that matter, when writing that the goal of the amendment would be to regain the affection of Catalans to the constitution (2017: 77). Secessionism can indeed decline, as has happened in Québec. In the October 2018 elections in Québec secessionist parties (*Québec Solidaire* and *Parti Québécois*) got 33% of the votes (similar to their combined result in the 2014 elections but far from the 49% they got in the 1995 referendum, and took only 19 seats—in 2014 they had 31). And according to polls, 20 years after the 1995 referendum in which secession got 49.4% of the votes, 82% of respondents of a prestigious survey in Québec agreed with the statement "*Ultimately, Québec should stay in Canada*" (73% of francophone respondents said Québec should remain in Canada and considered settled the sovereignty issue).[11]

The "nation" issue is indeed a very relevant matter for Catalan nationalism, and has for many decades had an extremely important symbolic value, and a very prominent political significance. Thus, in the constitutional period started in 1978, and much before the secessionist process started, the main demand of the more nationalist Catalan leaders was the recognition of Catalonia as a nation (although it was not openly said whether this would mean an entitlement for independence). As I explained before (see Chapter 1, Sect. 3), the nullification by the Constitutional Court of a provision of the 2006 "*Estatuto*" which stated—without actual legal force—that Catalonia considered itself a

---

[10] See http://www.psoe.es/propuestas/reforma-constitucional/.

[11] See https://www.cbc.ca/news/canada/montreal/Québec-angus-reid-canada-indepdence-1.3788110.

nation was received by Catalan leaders as a *casus belli*. So symbolically and politically, a constitutional reform which would explicitly acknowledge that Catalonia is a nation could be very important.

I do believe that taking steps towards this recognition would very much persuade secessionists—at least the less radical—to accept the constitutional framework and to abandon the bid for independence. If one of the triggering facts of the secessionist process was the barring of the mention that of Catalonia is a nation, then retracing steps in this aspect will be a wise thing to do. But this poses at least two main problems. The first one is that in Spain, contrary to the UK, accepting that some territories are a nation has a negative, perilous connotation. I do not intend to mean that it is a justified worry, but the truth is that from a historical point of view, during the First (1873) and the Second Republic (1931–1939) the claim of territorial nations led to chaos and to attempts of secession, mainly but not only in Catalonia. The second issue is that expressly admitting that Catalonia is a nation seems to be not compatible with article 2 of the constitution, which reads "*the Constitution is based on the indissoluble unity of the Spanish Nation*". So, as the Constitutional Court said in its 42/2014 judgement, under the constitution there can be only one nation.

The first problem is a political one (even psychological) and might be solved with persuasion, realism, and only if the notions of "nation" and "secession" are decoupled. Actually, other countries such as the UK use the word and the concept of "nation" and this is not detrimental to the unity of the common "nation". And for example France uses the word "*pays*" ("country") to refer to territories or regions, and it does so without fear of secession. Indeed, appealing to the wording of some appellations and names might be revealing. When article 2 of the constitution states that Spain is unitarian and indivisible and formed of "nationalities and regions", to me it is clear that these "nationalities" (among them, Catalonia), actually do contain the essence of a nation. Admitting that Catalonia, or the Basque Country, are nations within a plurinational Spain should not be considered as the end of a united Spain, if the concept of "nation" is properly, openly and unprejudicially interpreted, and in any case without the stigmas of a now very distant past. Actually, as Caamaño says (2014: 243), admitting that Spain is a plurinational nation would reflect reality. And might not be detrimental for the essential collective identity of Spain because it would still be a nation, an indivisible nation indeed—but made of other nations.

The second problem is a legal one. A constitutional clear mention of Catalonia, and maybe other nationalities, as nations would be considered incompatible with article 2 of the constitution. So it would need to me amended. As Tornos Mas has pointed out (2017: 77), a constitutional amendment which would expressly state that Spain is not *one* indivisible nation but is a "nation of nations" would very probably require the "hard" or "extraordinary" process of article 168, which, as was said, is extremely burdensome. But definitely it is not an impossible endeavor, provided that it is made clear that the recognition of "internal nations" does not equate to entitling them to the right of self-determination or to become independent.

Returning to reform proposals, Caamaño (2014) also suggests a federalist amendment. He coincides with the experts' report of 2017 in the general idea of federalizing Spain, but his proposal deepens the federal traits. According to his view, adding federalist features without creating a true federation is a "soft" arrangement which might temporarily heal the wounds but would hardly cure the malady—that is, might not solve the problem of territorial self-government or of the acceptance of the constitutional framework. Caamaño goes further and advocates a real federation non just in a technical way but also—and more importantly—in a political, even moral way. He sees the federation, maybe a little too much platonically, as "a commitment of loyalty to the system and to the other parts of the country [...] which requires federal culture, and a profound sense of democracy, of faithfulness and of responsibility" (2014: 186). Although Caamaño is not very specific about which one of the processes (the "hard" one or the "soft" one) would be needed to implement his deep federal reform, probably the hard one of article 168 would be applied—particularly because he advocates for a plurinational Spain, which clearly would require amending article 2. This would make the operation much more complex from a legal point of view and much more uncertain from a political standpoint.

Both the "soft" federalism of Muñoz Machado, Tornos and the scholar's group which would not need to trigger the "hard" amendment process of article 168, and the "hard" or "real" federalism" advocated by Caamaño rely in the persuasive virtues and in symbolic contents—the recognition of "nations". Any of them can calm down secessionist feelings, or make the moderate secessionists feel at ease with the new situation, and persuade them to remain as a part of a federal, perhaps "plurinational" Spain. Any non-divisive, well-explained and seriously debated constitutional reform might in practical terms be the only chance to appease or perhaps to solve the Catalan secessionist problem. And this is why in my opinion these proposals (in either modality "soft" or "hard") are extremely important.

Under all these proposals lies the hope that democratic federalism would be able to assimilate or to encompass both the "state" nationalism and the peripheral nationalisms. Keeping unity (though establishing a common *demos*) while respecting some plurality and diversity has from decades been the Arcadia of the federalist political theory, and the reason why it has recently been considered a possible solution to the Catalan conflict might be that it has never been tested in Spain. This might explain why all these scholars and politicians so optimistically advocate federalism as a possible solution.

Given the divisive political climate in Catalonia, it remains to be seen if this kind of reform would appease secessionists, even the non-radicals, for it would not permit a referendum on secession, nor establish a procedure for secession. Moreover, as for now the odds for a deal on the reform between the Socialist party and the Popular party are clearly against. The attitude of Prime Minister Sánchez towards constitutional reform—which necessarily requires an agreement at least with the Popular Party—is another factor which makes it difficult to be optimistic. In September 2018 he announced that his government would launch a constitutional reform aimed at eliminating or limiting procedural privileges for politicians and other public officials subject to trial. It was a non-agreed, previously undebated announcement, almost frivolous, and was made in a party meeting. The reform has almost no chance to come to fruition, and it looked like as if for Mr. Sánchez constitutional reforms were one more among the many proclamations politicians ordinarily make. Additionally, the Popular Party's attitude is not promising regarding some kind of agreement. Its new leader, Mr. Pablo Casado, during question time in October 2018 accused Prime Minister Sánchez of being accomplice to what he called the "Catalan coup" (*"golpe de estado"*).[12]

To me, in contemporary Spain what is to be feared is not just Catalan secessionism. What is to be feared is rather this kind of theatrical, confrontational politics, rooted in peevishness, short-termism and rancor,

---

[12] See https://www.theguardian.com/world/2018/oct/25/honeymoon-over-for-spain-socialists-as-rivals-seize-on-scandals.

which makes it extremely difficult to reach essential agreements and to leave aside selfish drives. But, as I said before, all these negative features of politics were mostly overcame and left aside during the Transition. So there is no reason to believe that we Spaniards cannot do it again.

5.3 Is There Really No Space for Some Kind of Agreed Referendum?

From a legal standpoint there seem to be only two options to deal with the Catalan secessionist problem: a complete constitutional reform which would make it legal the "right to decide" (and therefore to hold a referendum on independence and to secede from Spain) and a partial, "federalizing" constitutional reform which would appease some of the supporters of secession. But there exists a chink. It consists in an idea launched by Rubio Llorente in two op-eds in *EL PAÍS* (2012, 2013a). Rubio Llorente can fairly be considered the most important and prestigious constitutional law judge and scholar in Spain the last 70 years, and his thesis consists in affirming that it would not be contrary to the Constitution if the national government allowed holding a referendum in Catalonia:

> If a minoritarian part of the population of a specific territory (that is, not spread across the Nation, as happens in some countries in western Europe), administratively demarcated and with a dimension and resources a priori sufficient to become a State, wants to be independent, the democratic principle impedes to block or to deny this will by opposing legal and formal obstacles which can be removed. If the constitution forbids this solution (which I believe is not the case), then we should change it, but before that we should explore if this will actually exist and if its solid. (2012)

So he believes there exists some legal margin which would allow the national government to hold some kind of referendum in Catalonia regarding its political status and its relationship with Spain. Actually, Rubio Llorente is not the only Spanish scholar who spoke out in favor of some kind of flexibility aimed at holding a referendum: see Ruiz Robledo (2012), de Carreras (2012), and partially Caamaño (2014: 236 ff.), defending the constitutionality, and the necessity, of "exploring other ways", as they said, and concluding that article 92 of the constitution would allow the national parliament to call for a referendum in Catalonia.

According to Rubio Llorente, only relatively small, legal—not constitutional—obstacles can impede to the national government to hold an "exploratory consultation" or referendum in Catalonia. Being a power granted only to national authorities, the Catalan government cannot call for the referendum unilaterally, nor organize it, but it should be legally and politically allowed to ask for it and the national government should also be legally, constitutionally and politically allowed to accept the bid, to negotiate the terms of a referendum, and to call for it. This means that the referendum would be necessarily agreed between national government and Catalan government, and it would be not just fully constitutional, it would also be politically advisable: "*The Catalan people has the right to express its will, and this expression should be taken into account by the national authorities and by the Spanish people as a whole, but Catalan people has no right to impose it*" (Rubio Llorente 2013b). It would not be a referendum on more powers (such as the ones held in Veneto and Lombardy in 2017: see Chapter 2, Sect. 3.2), it would not be a referendum for a new "*Estatuto*", it would not be a referendum on independence as the ones held in Québec and in Scotland (at least the question would not be yes/no to independence). It would be an exploratory consultation or test on the will of Catalans regarding its political and institutional relationship with Spain, and would be non-binding from a strictly constitutional perspective.

This idea launched as early as 2012 is not only contrary to what the Constitutional Court would later decide in judgement 42/2014, it is also contrary to the mainstream ideas among constitutional law scholars, according to which any kind of possible consultation or referendum having to do with secession is prohibited. For example Aláez (2015: 149), without expressly mentioning Rubio Llorente's proposal, rules it out when he argues that under the Spanish constitutional system there is no room for a "third way" between stagnation or do-nothing policy, and the constitutionalization of the right to secession. More nuancedly, the 2017 experts report states that "some less traumatic possibilities than a referendum on independence" should be explored (Muñoz Machado 2017: 9), apparently implying, for instance, that a consultation on a new institutional framework for self-government, or on the relationship with Spain, might be acceptable. But the report says that this would require a previous constitutional reform and therefore pertains to the orthodox approach to the issue according to which the existing constitution forbids a regional referendum on secession-related matters. This makes the report very different from Rubio Llorente's idea.

Despite of the fact that Rubio Llorente's proposal is overwhelmingly considered contrary to the constitution, in my opinion it is a realistic suggestion, mainly because it does not require a previous constitutional reform. From this point of view, the proposal is relatively similar to the Canadian model, in which the referendum can be held without a previous constitutional amendment, and only if secession prevails—and with a clear majority—then negotiations would start in order to amend the constitution for allowing the secession of the territory. Rubio Llorente's thesis is not just realistic and much quicker than a constitutional amendment to allow the referendum. To me, it might fit into the constitution, particularly in the regulation of referenda contained in article 92—not stringently construed. Article 92 reads that

> 1. Political decisions of special importance may be submitted to all citizens in a consultative referendum. 2. The referendum shall be called by the King on the President of the Government's proposal after previous authorization by the Congress. 3. An organic bill shall lay down the terms and procedures for the different kinds of referendum provided for in this Constitution.

According to Rubio Llorente, the organic bill (*"ley orgánica"*) at Sect. 3, after being amended by the national parliament, could allow and regulate referenda in which *"all citizens"* would not need be the whole Spanish electorate but the specific electorate of a particular territory. This, Rubio Llorente believes, and also apparently do the other scholars which advocate for a referendum (Ruiz Robledo, de Carreras), would not contradict the unitarian sovereignty of the Spanish people solemnly mentioned in article 2 of the constitution. A more nuanced, orthodox position has been maintained by Caamaño (2014). He contends the need for a referendum, but not *à la* Rubio Llorente, which he deems contrary to article 92, but rather through a partial constitutional amendment which would not need to be channelled through the almost impossible path of article 168, as the Constitutional Court has suggested, but would consist in amending, precisely, article 92 for allowing territorial referenda. Caamaño writes (2014: 240) that this would make it legal a "clear" referendum, and would be equivalent to an agreement which would be "the Spanish Clarity Act"—although it is clear that, as was explained in Chapter 2, Sect. 2.1, and as Romero Caro suggests (2017: E140), the Canadian model is not just an agreed referendum, for its main aspect consists in the negotiations that would follow a hypothetic victory of secession. Tornos Mas (2017: 76) envisages this possibility, and concedes that it has the virtue of being pragmatic, but casts doubt regarding its compatibility with the constitution (he writes that the amendment would still provoke that a single territory would decide over the whole nation and this would violate the national sovereignty of article 2).

Having said that, I am perfectly aware of the problems Rubio Llorente's proposal entails. First, it would not be easy to persuade the unionist political leaders to allow a referendum in Catalonia, but perhaps it might be easier than persuading them to initiate the extremely burdensome amendment procedure of article 168 of the constitution—which is the other possibility of allowing a referendum. Second, the momentum of a hypothetical referendum à la Rubio Llorente would have been 2013 or 2014, before the political climate had become so harsh. Hence, holding a referendum in the current divisive, partisan, hooligan-like political scenario might not help to find a solution. And third, as Martinico (2018) has pointed out, democratic referenda on identitarian issues might deepen division and exclusion instead of clearing up the horizon—although Caamaño (2014: 229) writes that "the matter is so serious that it requires certainties and convictions. Referendum is the only instrument that can bring them". Certainly, referenda are not without problems, and might for sure exacerbate the social and political split, particularly if the question is not "clear" and the surrounding issues are not candidly and in good faith brought to the table. But in Spain and in Catalonia, as I just said, we already have this social and political split, so I do not think a hypothetical referendum would make things worse.

If Rubio Llorente's proposal is unpersuasive, or is considered incompatible with article 92 of the constitution, then Caamaño's suggestion of amending this article and then holding the referendum might be easier to accept by national parties and by the Constitutional Court. Any of these ideas might actually be the only realistic chances—if any—of channeling a possible solution to the secessionist problem. By pointing out that an agreed referendum would not necessarily be contrary to the constitution, Rubio Llorente at least might have helped to break the deadlock or would have initiated a debate, a serious one, on the need for a referendum. And, because it tries to interpret the constitution in an open, flexible fashion, it could be considered consistent with Nicolaïdis idea (2017) that governments should use the law to create spaces for the full expression of all opinions. Unfortunately, Rubio Lorente died in January 2016 and he could not be part of the ongoing debate. Indeed, Aláez's, Plaza's and other's ideas are fair constitutional interpretations. Sticking, as they do, to the formalistic vision of the constitution is undoubtedly correct, but being legally correct does not mean being politically useful, or viable in the long run.

Even taking into account Rubio's or Caamaño's proposals, it is not easy to give an optimistic prognosis. At least if one believes, as Keating argues (2015: 13) referring to Québec, Scotland and Catalonia, that competing conceptions of sovereignty, of political community and identity can never be resolved once and for all. If, accordingly, the definition of the boundaries of the political community, that is, the *demos*, is clearly a pre-legal and pre-constitutional matter, and if modern, occidental democracies are not able to integrate Scots, Québecers and Catalans in a pluralistic, decentralized constitutional system, then Keating might be right, and a complete resolution to the Catalan problem would hardly occur.

6   Final Reflections

From a constitutional point of view, the problem recently emerged in Spain because of the secessionist movement fostered by almost half of the population and of the regional political parties of Catalonia has no easy solution—or no solution at all—in federal countries, and in non-federal countries as well. The constitutions of the most important federal models (the US, Mexico, Australia, Germany, Canada, Brazil, Argentina, South Africa) do not allow the states or provinces to secede. Regarding not secession but a referendum on secession the situation is also quite clear: under the existing Spanish legal framework Catalonia has not the possibility to have a Scottish-Canadian-style referendum (because, pursuant to the mainstream constitutional interpretation, the national government has not the right nor the power to authorize it, or if there is to be a referendum it should be held at national level). Accordingly, Catalonia has not the right to initiate through a referendum a secession process aimed at becoming and independent state. Only a constitutional amendment could give way to a referendum, and therefore could channel, in a *Canadian* way, the secessionist process. But this reform which would allow secession is, in my opinion, extremely unlikely to be achieved.

Social and political unrest is growing in Spain, and much more in Catalonia. From a strictly political perspective, four of the last five terms of the Catalan Parliament did not last the ordinary pre-established four-year period (Presidents Maragall and Mas—twice—called early elections, and Mr. Rajoy dissolved the Catalan Parliament when his government implemented direct rule in October 2017). And the Catalan social situation is starting to be worrisome. The Catalan society was quite homogenous, had a long tradition of integrating immigrants from other parts of Spain, and until 2010 was relatively non-porous to the divisive feature of the radical nationalist or secessionist agenda pushed by *Esquerra* (and from that year also by *Convergencia*). But since the secessionist process was triggered, Catalan society has started to shift to division and to confrontation. Lluís Bassets, a prestigious Catalan journalist and then-deputy director of *EL PAÍS*, wrote (2017) that "*Everything seems ready to transform Catalonia in some kind of Ulster, without arms yet, in which two communities already split, uncommunicated and enemies are forced to a coexistence full of pain and resentment and, in short, of hate*". As I said before, this seems to me the saddest aspect: bitterness and unrest, and even growing hatred—and sometimes verbal violence and threats—have spread in Catalonia in many social groups and in factories, schools, universities, journalism, municipalities, etc.

Other aspects of society have also become deteriorated. Both governments (national and Catalan) have politically used the police, and the media, and have seemingly put undue pressure on judges and prosecutors. Mr. Rajoy seemed to decline any kind of responsibility and, after an ad hoc amendment to the bill regulating the Constitutional Court, relied completely on it to tackle the secessionist challenge. This was clearly detrimental to the prestige and the *auctoritas* of the Court, for, as Urías writes (2017), it looked as if it was taking part in the political controversy and was assuming a partisan role. I would not be as pessimistic as Urías when he argues that the Constitutional Court is on the path of self-destruction, mainly because its eventual destruction would have been caused by others, and not by the Court itself (although it is not completely free of guilt). But he might be right when he stresses the serious loss of credibility of the Court.

More broadly, the partisan use of law and of the constitution has of course its downsides. First, an institutional deterioration, which I just mentioned regarding the Constitutional Court, and which is particularly severe in Catalonia, because almost all the institutions (courts, parliament, media, universities, banks and corporations, etc.) were put in the middle of the battlefield. As Roig (2017) has showed, the Constitutional Court case law regarding Catalan secession has had negative "reciprocal impacts" on other fields of the public sphere, and they might last for a long time. And second, Galán (2014: 907) sees a risk of "turning back the clock to times in which law was not conceived a useful way of solving social conflicts but as a domination instrument or as a tool of sheer power". Perhaps Galán is exaggerating, but we should not forget that Spain has a short tradition of democracy, rule of law and human rights, and therefore that, as he warns, we should not overlook the fact that opposing law and democracy is a risky thing in young democracies.

There is another reason to feel gloomy. We Spaniards were, and many still are, in general proud of our Transition and of the 1978 constitution—despite of some serious flaws in the political system such as political corruption, lack of transparency and accountability, a clearly improvable independence of the judiciary, and excessive power of political parties. One of the main successes of the constitutional regime was to accommodate self-government claims of the so-called "historic nationalities" (Catalonia, Basque Country and Galicia—and maybe also Navarre and apparently also Andalusia), and even to all the territories (see Chapter 1, Sect. 2, and the so-called "*café para todos*"). Overcoming many hurdles, the constitution and the politicians of that time dealt very quickly (from 1978 to 1983) with the territorial problem, and this was without any doubt a historical success. This was the first time since the first Spanish constitution (in 1812) that democracy, rule of law, and human rights were peacefully, democratically and long-lastingly granted after an overwhelming political deal, and particularly that the territorial problem was democratically settled. Well, this is not so anymore, at least regarding Catalonia. The "Catalan problem" has revived, and half of the population of Catalonia does not seem to feel bound anymore by the constitutional pact. The constitutional and political Spanish system, and part of the Spanish society, has shifted from inclusion and consensus to confrontation based on exclusive nationalisms, and hence many Spaniards have something like an indefinite, bitter sensation of failure.

My impression is that this failure is also perceived by Catalans, both non-secessionists and probably also secessionists. The latter supported the proclamation a Republic which did not even exist, and were bluffed by a generation of political leaders which played irresponsibly with coexistence and brought division and conflict with almost nothing to offer in return. Secessionists also saw how the EU openly turned back on them. On the other hand, non-secessionists feel, with good reason, pointed at as bad Catalans and somewhat stigmatized. They are indeed victims of exclusive nationalism. To me, all Catalans, secessionists or not, are victims of exclusive nationalism. All Catalans have good arguments to believe that Catalonia is in 2018 worse, in many aspects, than it was in 2006, and not just because of the economic crisis.

The rebirth of secessionism in fully democratic countries is a problem that has arisen in the last two or three decades in some plurinational (or pluricultural) federations such as Canada, the UK, and also Belgium, India, and now Spain. Some scholars (see Keating 2012: 13) stress that the federalist constitutional and political theory is not suited to facing or to solving nationalistic issues. In fact this can be said of every constitutional theory. In this sense, nationalism is usually considered the Achilles' heel of federalism. Constitutional asymmetries or political differentiations, as there exist for instance in the EU, are possible solutions, but they rely heavily on the acceptation by nationalisms of a minimal collective space, and of a minimal sense of belonging to a common *demos*. Again, these are psychological factors or sentiments, and in general they are not connected to law or to constitutional theory. Integrating in a common legal framework territorial nationalisms has been historically the main challenge of Constitutional federalism, and now of the EU, and is presently put to the test in Spain.

But, paradoxically enough, a specific aspect of nationalism might help to solve or at least to appease the Catalan conflict. As I mentioned earlier, in the contemporary democratic period in Spain the quintessential claim of Catalan nationalists has been that "*We are a nation*", and between 2010 and 2012 this transformed into "*We want to be an independent nation*", triggering the secessionist process. Well, if this is the main problem, and if it still time, the constitutional recognition of Catalonia as a nation within a plurinational Spain would likely satisfy a relevant part of secessionists. If, despite the considerable hurdles, this would work, Spain would have successfully combatted nationalism with nationalism. I mean that Spain would have used the symbolic, somewhat irrational identitarian features of nationalism to keep its unity and, in my opinion, to be more inclusive and to strengthen itself.

At any event, it is legitimate to be skeptical about the place, and the justification, that nationalism can have in a highly globalized world, particularly in the EU, which is the most globalized part of the planet. Moreover, it is a sad fact, as Weiler states: *"It is ethically demoralizing to see the likes of Catalonia reverting to an early 20th-century post-World War I mentality, when the notion that a single state could encompass more than one nationality seemed impossible"* (2012: 910); *"The case for independence [...] is precisely that notion that having a distinct national identity justifies secession, a notion fueled in my view by a seriously misdirected social and economic egoism, cultural and national hubris and the naked ambition of local politicians"* (Weiler 2014). In a world in which sovereignty is disappearing Weiler, and many others, find it difficult to understand why Scots and Catalans have revived the myths of the nation, and of sovereignty. The truth is that in the last 30 years nationalist tendencies have appeared in Europe (Weiler refers to it as "euro-tribalism"). By nationalist tendencies I do not mean just secessionist movements: I am referring also to some reactions of right wing parties such as the bizarre creation by President Sarkozy in 2007 of a Ministry in charge of "national identity" (Ministère de l'Immigration, de l'Intégration et de l'Identité Nationale), and to the more recent rise of powerful right-wing populisms in Italy, Hungary, Belgium, Austria, Poland or France, and to a lesser extent—with between 10 and 15 % of voter support—in Sweden, Germany or the Netherlands. This has put again into question both the idea of the nation-state and the frontiers established in the nineteenth century (in the Vienna Congress in 1815) and in the twentieth century (in the Versailles Treaty, after WW II and after the collapse of communist régimes). Apart from the peaceful secession of Czechoslovakia and of the Baltic Republics there are some examples of how Europe continues to have trouble to adjust its frontiers and to settle national cultural identities. I am referring to some Russian republics—and lately to Ukraine, of course—to Scotland, Northern Ireland, Spain, Cyprus, Belgium and, to a lesser extent, Corsica and the north of Italy, which are territories which have different levels of nationalistic drives. The future of the EU, and the idea which lies at its very basis (to overcome not just war but also frontiers, nationalism and the less attractive aspect of sovereignty) might certainly be at risk if sovereigntism, parochialism, nationalism (actually, national-populism, which usually leads to euro-skepticism) start to spread.

I will finish quoting one of the most important Catalan journalists of all times, Mr. Agustí Calvet Pascual *"Gaziel"* (1887–1964), director of the main newspaper of Barcelona (*La Vanguardia*) from 1920 to 1936. During the Second Republic (1931–1939), and in the aftermath of the

Catalan "*Estatuto*" of 1932 and the insurrection led by the Catalan government which proclaimed the Catalan State in 1934, he wrote:

> Few peoples in the world have had so favorable circumstances, or have had so favorable momentum and situation to make real their political dreams and aspirations. After the end of the monarchy and the Estatuto de Autonomía of 1932, Catalonia was one of them, within the Spanish brotherhood (Gaziel 2013: 277) [...] The Estatuto is the first serious attempt made by the Spaniards to give Catalonia the soul it was looking for. The first try of this dress has been a disaster, and has ended with the dress in tatters [*the author is referring to the independence declaration of October 1934 and to the prosecution and imprisonment of Catalan leaders*]. Let's not forget that this soul, wild and brave, is seriously disturbed by a long and painful decorporisation. We need to calm it and bring it little by little, with infinite patience, to a normal situation within an adequate body, after hysterical adventures of a vagabond soul. There is nothing to gain if, instead of appeasing this wandering soul, we infuriate and torture it. (Gaziel 2013: 270, author's translation)

Gaziel finishes stating (2013: 276) that Catalans alone were to blame, and that everything was lost (the title of the book, in Catalan, is "*Tot s'ha perdut*"—*All Is lost*).

REFERENCES

Aláez Corral, Benito. 2015. Constitucionalizar la secesión para armonizar la legalidad constitucional y el principio democrático en Estados territorialmente descentralizados como España. *Revista de Estudios Autonómicos y Federales* (22): 136–183.

Bassets, Lluís. 2017. Mundos que se alejan. *EL PAÍS*, December 11. https://politica.elpais.com/politica/2017/12/10/aixo_va_de_democracia_blog_contra_llo/1512946678_084298.html.

Caamaño, Francisco. 2014. *Democracia federal: Apuntes sobre España*. Madrid: Ediciones Turpial.

Closa, Carlos. 2016. Secession from a Member State and EU Membership: The View from the Union. *European Constitutional Law Review* 12 (2): 240–264.

De Carreras, Francesc. 2012. ¿Un referéndum? *La Vanguardia*, September 20. https://www.lavanguardia.com/opinion/articulos/20120920/54350587199/francesc-de-carreras-un-referendum.html.

Ferreres Comella, Victor, Enric Fossas, and Alejandro Sáiz Arnáiz. 2017. Las trece campanadas del soberanismo. *EL PAÍS*, March 21. https://elpais.com/elpais/2017/03/16/opinion/1489692590_562601.html.

Fossas Espadaler, Enric. 2014. Secesión: del proceso eufemístico al constitucional. *EL PAÍS*, November 25. http://elpais.com/elpais/2014/11/24/opinion/1416842833_782695.html.

Galán Galán, Alfredo. 2014. Del derecho a decidir a la independencia: la peculiaridad del proceso secesionista en Cataluña. *Istituzioni del Federalismo* 4: 885–907.

Gaziel. 2013. *Tot s'ha perdut*, Biblioteca del catalanisme, RBA, Barcelona—Used by permission.

González, Felipe. 2015. A los catalanes. *EL PAÍS*, August 30. http://elpais.com/elpais/2015/08/29/opinion/1440863481_811526.html.

Keating, Michael. 2012. Rethinking Sovereignty. Independence-lite, Devolution-Max and National Accommodation. *Revista de Estudios Autonómicos y Federales* 16: 9–29.

Keating, Michael. 2015. The Scottish Independence Referendum and After. *Revista de Estudios Autonómicos y Federales* 21: 73–98.

Linera, Presno, and A. Miguel. 2015. Law and Disagreement: el 'caso de Cataluña en España'. *Diritto Pubblico* 1: 63–84.

López Bofill, Héctor. 2018. Hubris, Constitutionalism, and 'The Indissoluble Unity of the Spanish Nation'. The Repression of Catalan Secessionist Referenda in Spanish Constitutional Law'. *I.CON. International Journal of Constitutional Law* 17 (forthcoming).

Martinico, Giuseppe. 2018. How Can Constitutionalism Deal with Secession in the Age of Populism? The Case of Referendums. *Sant'Anna Legal Studies—STALS Research Paper 5/2018*. http://www.stals.sssup.it/files/martinico%205%202018%20stals.pdf.

Muñoz Machado, Santiago. 2014. *Cataluña y las demás Españas*. Madrid: Crítica.

Muñoz Machado, Santiago. 2016. *Vieja y nueva Constitución*. Madrid: Crítica.

Muñoz Machado, Santiago (ed.). 2017. Ideas para una reforma de la constitución. http://idpbarcelona.net/docs/actual/ideas_reforma_constitucion.pdf.

Nicolaïdis, Kalypso. 2017. Catalonia and the Theatres of Recognition. https://www.opendemocracy.net/can-europe-make-it/kalypso-nicola-dis/catalonia-and-theaters-of-recognition.

Plaza, Carmen. 2018. Catalonia's Secession Process at the Constitutional Court: A Never-Ending Story? *European Public Law* 24 (3): 373–392.

Ridao, Joan, and Alfonso González Bondía. 2014. La unión europea ante la eventual creación de nuevos estados surgidos de la secesión de estados miembros. *Revista de Derecho de la Unión Europea* 27: 363–390.

Roig i Molés, Eduard. 2017. The Catalan Sovereignty Process and the Spanish Constitutional Court. An Analysis of Reciprocal Impacts. *Revista Catalana de Dret Públic* 54: 24–61.

Romano, Andrea. 2018. Constituent Power and Independence Processes: Problems and Perspectives in the Light of the Catalan Experience. *Revista de Estudios Autonómicos y Federales* 27: 41–79.

Romero Caro, Francisco Javier. 2017. The Spanish Vision of Canada's Clarity Act: From Idealization to Myth. *Perspectives on Federalism* 9 (3): E-133–E-159. http://www.on-federalism.eu/index.php/component/content/article/231-essay/273-the-spanish-vision-of-canadas-clarity-act-from-idealization-to-myth.

Rubio Llorente, Francisco. 2012. Un referéndum para Cataluña. *EL PAÍS*, October 8. http://elpais.com/elpais/2012/10/03/opinion/1349256731_659435.html.

Rubio Llorente, Francisco. 2013a. Un referéndum que nadie quiere. *EL PAÍS*, February 11. http://elpais.com/elpais/2013/02/01/opinion/1359716070_365196.html.

Rubio Llorente, Francisco. 2013b. Un referéndum, pero no cualquier referéndum. https://www.ahorasemanal.es/un-referendum,-pero-no-cualquier-referendum.

Ruiz Robledo, Agustín. 2012. Una respuesta canadiense a la cuestión catalana. *EL PAÍS*, October 30.

Sáiz Arnáiz, Alejandro. 2006–2007. Constitución y secesión. *Parlamento y Constitución. Anuario* 10: 33–56.

Sarmiento, Daniel. 2018. The Strange (German) Case of Mr. Puigdemont's European Arrest Warrant. https://verfassungsblog.de/the-strange-german-case-of-mr-puigdemonts-european-arrest-warrant/.

Tornos Mas, Joaquín. 2014. El problema catalán: una solución razonable. *El Cronista del Estado Social y Democrático de Derecho* 42: 44–53.

Tornos Mas, Joaquín. 2015. *De Escocia a Cataluña. Referéndum y reforma constitucional*. Madrid: Iustel.

Tornos Mas, Joaquín. 2017. Tras los hechos del primero de octubre, una nueva, y tal vez última, llamada al acuerdo dentro del Estado de Derecho. *El Cronista del Estado Social y Democrático de Derecho* 71–72: 74–77.

Urías, Joaquín. 2017. The Spanish Constitutional Court on the Path of Self-Destruction. VerfBlog, April 24. https://verfassungsblog.de/the-spanish-constitutional-court-on-the-path-of-self-destruction/.

Vidmar, Jure. 2017. Catalonia: The Way Forward Is Comparative Constitutional Rather Than International Legal Argument. https://www.ejiltalk.org/author/jvidmar/.

Vilajosana, Josep Maria. 2014. The Democratic Principle and Constitutional Justification of the Right to Decide. *Revista de Estudios Autonómicos y Federales* 19: 178–210.

Walker, Neil. 2015. *Internal Enlargement in the European Union: Beyond Legalism and Political Expediency*. Edinburgh School of Law Research Paper No. 2015/32; Europa Working Paper No. 2015/05. Available at SSRN: https://ssrn.com/abstract=2676025 and http://dx.doi.org/10.2139/ssrn.2676025 (later in Carlos Closa [ed.]. 2017. *Secession from a Member*

State and Withdrawal from the European Union: Troubled Membership, 32–47. Cambridge: Cambridge University Press).

Weiler, Joseph H.H. 2012. Editorial: Catalonian Independence and the European Union. *The European Journal of International Law* 23 (4): 910–912.

Weiler, Joseph H.H. 2014. Scotland and the EU: A Comment. *UK Constitutional Law Association*. https://ukconstitutionallaw.org/2014/09/10/debate-j-h-h-weiler-scotland-and-the-eu-a-comment/.

INDEX

Printed by Printforce, the Netherlands